Faith in 'Bomb City'

Ben Forde
with Chris Spencer

Marshalls

Marshalls Paperbacks
Marshall Pickering
3 Beggarwood Lane, Basingstoke,
Hants, RG23 7LP, UK

Unless otherwise stated, all biblical quotes are taken
from The Living Bible

Cover: Belfast Docks. Photo by Jim Lavery.
Inset photo: courtesy of the *Daily Mail*.

ISBN 0 551 01145 9

Typeset by Alan Sutton Publishing Ltd., Gloucester
Printed in Great Britain by Anchor Brendon Ltd.,
Tiptree, Colchester.

Contents

I dedicate this book

In loving memory of Mum
To Dad, who hunted with his son
And to Emily, my stepmother and much more

Acknowledgements

I wish to express my appreciation of my many friends within the Royal Ulster Constabulary, particularly those like Sid O'Connor (squad instructor) and Jim Lavery (squad-mate) whom I've known these past twenty-five years. To you all I say thanks for your comradeship and friendship.

Thanks are also due to Derick Bingham for his words of counsel and encouragement.

And to those within prison walls and without who have prayed for God's blessing upon the 'Bomb City' books, and upon the many who have read and shared these stories of hope, love and faith.

For obvious reasons some of the
names in this book have been changed.

1: Death threat

My home in South Belfast is situated in an area known as the Lagan Valley Regional Park, a belt of protected natural beauty covering many square miles of lovely parkland, waterway and forest. This is a side of Belfast that quietly contradicts the news media's image of 'Bomb City', for in stark contrast to the rubble-strewn streets with their rioting gangs, here the one who cares to look will find the stuff that dreams are made of. There are gardens to stroll in, woods to explore, river paths to follow, and high places where visitors may just sit and enjoy the view. All this – plus lashings of peace and quiet – just minutes from the bricked-up windows, the angry graffiti, and the gutters still wet with the latest victim's blood.

I'm no supercop. Fifteen years of fighting terrorism in Northern Ireland have not left me blasé – no way shall I ever get used to the debris of murder – and personally I *need* places like the Lagan Valley. The beauty, the tranquility bring a much-needed balance to the effects of living my life in the violent world of the IRA hit-man and his Loyalist counterpart. So, from time to time, I'll head out to some local beauty spot to snatch half an hour of sanity in my increasingly crazy world. Sometimes I'll take Shane, our restless red setter, and let him run his legs off chasing low-flying swallows; occasionally, Lily will pack up a picnic and we'll head for the hills with our teenage children, Keri and Clive, for a quiet lunch; and now and then, when the pressures dictate, I'll pull in to some public park just to be alone – to think, to breathe the air, and to pray.

The call had come through at two o'clock in the morning, jarring me from my sleep. Stiffly (the punishment for last night's game of squash) I propelled myself out of bed towards the phone – something of an automatic response, for over the years the call to duty has ruined many a good night's rest. I lifted the receiver and mumbled the number.

'Ben Forde?'

I fought off a yawn. 'Speaking.'

My caller identified himself as a police sergeant and gave the name of his station. He didn't apologise for dragging me out of bed; he didn't need to.

'I thought you ought to know, we've had word here that someone's out to nail you.'

Suddenly I was awake. 'Who wants me dead?'

'We don't know. All we heard is that you're to be killed on Saturday.'

My mind raced. What day was it today? Friday.

For a minute or two I quizzed my caller for more details or clues as to who was saying such things about me, but he knew nothing further. Then I thanked him for letting me know and went back to bed.

Death threats are nothing new to policemen in Ulster; our lives are constantly on the line and we know it. But at least at such times a man finds out where his security lies. Lying back on my pillow, staring up into the darkness, I wrestled with the dark message for a minute or two, then I prayed a prayer that's passed my lips more times than I can remember.

Lord, you got me into this; you're going to have to get me out of it.

I've been a Christian three years longer than I've been a policeman. I was sixteen years old when I realised my need of the Saviour and committed my life to him. When I signed up with the RUC (Royal Ulster Constabulary)

10

shortly before my nineteenth birthday, it was with a very real sense of God's leading; a sense that he wanted me in the police force not only to serve the community, but also to serve him.

At the time I could not have imagined what lay ahead of me. Though the IRA were active, most of the trouble in those days was confined to the border areas, and never could I have imagined that the years to come would see the monster called Terrorism rage across our land with such nightmarish ferocity.

But God knew. And, looking back, I now know why he spoke such a powerful word to my heart only minutes before I left home for the RUC Training Depot at Enniskillen that cold, clear February morning back in 1960.

Mum had already packed my Bible that morning, so with time to spare before I went for the bus I picked up my sister Leah's book of daily Scripture readings where I read these words: 'Trust in the Lord with all thine heart and lean not unto thine own understanding. In all thy ways acknowledge him, and he shall direct thy paths.'

Those words were packed with wisdom – God's wisdom – and over the years, as I'd passed through one set of dangers after another, and as my work with the CID had taken me deeper and deeper into the dark labyrinth of terrorism, I'd had cause to recall those words again and again. I did so now, as I lay in my bed, knowing that the day after next someone planned to end my life.

It wasn't the first time the terror had come close. On more than one occasion I'd had known killers spit words of death into my face, and I'd had to deal with those threats in the same way.

'Trust in the Lord with all thine heart . . .'

I do, Lord, I prayed. *I trust you. My life is yours, you know that. My times are in your hands.*

'And lean not unto thine own understanding . . .'

I've given up trying to understand this sick world, anyway. I don't even pretend to any more.

'In all thy ways acknowledge him . . .'
Lord, you know how I've tried to do just that.
'And he shall direct thy paths.'
Thank you for your leading – and forgive me for the times when I've insisted on going my own foolish way. I really don't want to walk anyone's paths but yours.

And almost as an afterthought I added, *Please direct my paths on Saturday.*

And with that I went to sleep.

It wasn't fear that pursued me throughout Friday because you can't trust the Lord *and* fear man. But I was pursued just the same. It was a sort of gloom; a heaviness. I suppose it had been coming on all week. Monday had set the mood with the murder of yet another RUC colleague – this time an officer I'd once served with many years ago and still regarded as a friend.

Tuesday found me at the scene of another murder – a bombing this time, with all the grisly remains to look over in the search for evidence of the explosives.

On Wednesday I spent a fruitless day chasing inquiries in Belfast, talking to people who probably knew more than they were saying, but would not talk for fear of reprisals.

Thursday was taken up with giving evidence in court against a known terrorist – a man we'd been trying to put away for a long time – and watching that man walk free on the grounds of insufficient evidence.

No wonder I felt gloomy. The job was difficult enough at the best of times, but in a week like this I found myself asking what was the point of continuing against such seemingly unbeatable odds. For every one step forward we were taking three steps back. How could we ever win over terrorism if every avenue that opened up to us was eventually blocked?

And now, to top it all, someone had taken it into his head to put a bullet in mine.

It is not often that these things get me down, but on this occasion I began to wonder how ever I was going to

12

carry on. And it was in that frame of mind, on my way home from work that evening, that I swung off the road into one of the Lagan Valley's beautiful parks.

How was it possible to carry on in the face of such rampant evil? To my weary mind it seemed we were no nearer stemming the tide of violence than we were when the present troubles had begun back in 1969. What was the answer, Lord?

I left the car and headed through the trees to find a bench out of the blustery wind that was beating across the park. And it was there, sitting looking out across the valley, that the answer seemed to come.

As I'd sat down I'd become aware of a small bulk in my jacket pocket – a New Testament I'd been asked to obtain for a man presently being interviewed at Castlereagh Holding Centre about various terrorist offences. I'd hoped to see him that day to hand it to him, but duties had prevented the visit. Right now I was glad of that, for over the years God's Word had been a source of much comfort and inspiration during difficult times, and as I opened up the little book I sensed hope begin to rise within me.

Flicking through, I paused at one familiar chapter after another, but nothing seemed to gel with my present line of thought . . . until my eyes came to rest in Ephesians – St Paul's letter to the Christians at Ephesus. As I read, I realised that the Apostle might just as easily have been writing to the believers in Ulster, and especially to Christian policemen or soldiers. So much of our time was spent in pursuing a human enemy that at times, like these past few days, I completely forgot that there was another, more evil, more powerful enemy at work. With fresh enlightenment I read: 'We are not fighting against people made of flesh and blood, but against persons without bodies – the evil rulers of the unseen world, those mighty satanic beings and great evil princes of darkness who rule this world; and against huge numbers of wicked spirits in the spirit world.'

13

That was true – it had to be. Man alone could not be guilty of the sort of inhumanity to his brother that I'd witnessed that past week and throughout the years; there just had to be a greater evil driving him onward. The terrorist, though responsible for his own actions, was not accomplishing his own goal, for behind all evil was the evil one himself, Satan, and by committing murder the terrorist was simply allowing himself to be used.

I leaned back on the park bench, thankful for this reminder, for the Scriptures had put things in perspective for me. The real battle we faced in Northern Ireland was a spiritual one, and that battle, I knew, had already been won. Christ, on the cross, had routed Satan – defeated him utterly, eternally – and what we were seeing in the violence of the age was only the frustrated backlash of a conquered foe allowed a measure of liberty before being bound and thrown into that place prepared for him.

Yes, my God was the victor, and because I had placed my trust in him, I too was victorious. But not in my own strength. In Ephesians again I read: 'Your strength must come from the Lord's mighty power at work within you.'

The *weapons* of this warfare were God's too. Turning back to Corinthians, I found more words of Paul's that had sustained me in times past: 'It is true that I am an ordinary weak human being, but I don't use human plans and methods to win my battles. I use God's mighty weapons, not those made by men, to knock down the devil's strongholds.'

How would we beat terrorism? With 'God's mighty weapons'!

But was this pie in the sky? Was I only dreaming? Was the spiritual victory of any consequence in the all-too-real daily battle against men with murder on their minds? I could just imagine some of my colleagues tossing that one at me, but I did not need convincing of the answer: resoundingly, yes!

14

I read on: 'With these weapons I can capture rebels and bring them back to God, and change them into men whose hearts' desire is obedience to Christ.'

The answer, surely, was not to change the system, dream up settlements, employ initiatives, but to 'capture rebels' – not simply by physical means, but spiritually, with Christ's love. Things would change in Northern Ireland only when *men* changed. Peace would return to the Province only when men themselves were at peace with God.

I closed the little book and slipped it back into my pocket.

But that was going to take time; even someone who believed in miracles realised that! Many Christians, I knew, were working and praying to this end, and thankfully over the years we had seen a number of encouraging signs in this area, but it could be many years still before we would see the gospel actually reducing the level of violence. In the meantime we had to press on; we had to keep the faith.

Faith . . .

I let the word linger for a while, for therein lay the key to my peace – a peace that had returned, like a dove coming home to roost, during the few minutes I'd been sitting there with the Bible in the tranquil surroundings of the park.

Yes, it was my faith in Christ that made it possible for me to go on, for much as I loved Northern Ireland and was determined to work towards its peace, my sights were set on a much higher goal; a city where there would be no bombs, no heartache, not even so much as a teardrop.

I smiled to myself as I recalled the leg-pulling I'd received about this over the years. 'Ben, you're fooling yourself; when you're dead, you're dead. All this talk of heaven's just castles in the air.'

But my faith told me otherwise. How did the Bible describe faith? 'The confident assurance that something we want is going to happen; the certainty that what we hope for is waiting for us, even though we cannot see it up ahead.'

It was one of those spiritual mysteries that no one could explain, only experience. Either it was real to you or it wasn't, and personally I was thankful for it. Where would I be without my faith?

The thought stirred a memory, and reaching into my jacket I brought out a letter that had been waiting for me on my desk when I'd arrived at work that morning. It was from a lady in Castlereagh, Mrs Elizabeth Brown, who had written to me after reading *Love in 'Bomb City'*. In that Book, as well as in *Hope in 'Bomb City'*, I'd shared something of the pain and the preparation involved in leaving home after nineteen years to join the RUC. Apparently Mrs Brown identified with much of what I'd written – her own son, Mark, had left home to join the force just a few months earlier – and now she was writing to say how much she'd appreciated having the book to read at that time.

'It helped me as a mother through those long weeks of Mark's training,' she wrote, 'and I'm sure many other mothers would say the same thing.' I was glad to know that sharing some of my own experiences had been a comfort to Mrs Brown, but as I read through her letter for the second time that day it was the last paragraph that seemed to stand out: 'Surely your next book must be *Faith in 'Bomb City'*. Without faith, where would we be?'

The third book was already more than an idea in my head – and, yes, it *was* to be 'Faith' this time – but this letter spurred me on. When I went for the car there was something of a spring in my step. Gone was the gloom that had ridden with me to the park that evening; vanished was my despair over carrying on. All of that, I decided – including the threat on my life (which turned out to be a false alarm) – was part of the enemy's tactics to wear me down and to keep me from persevering in the work my God had laid before me. Part of that work was this book, and it really was time I set things moving.

After tea, I helped Lily wash up, played Monopoly with the kids for a while, and took Shane for a walk. But I really couldn't wait to get back.

Indoors, Lily was doing some sewing. 'Did you get that new ribbon for the typewriter?' I asked.

2: Writing in the dark

I suppose the seed for this book had been sown many months before, shortly after the publication of *Love in 'Bomb City'*. Even then, or perhaps earlier still, I had known there was a third book to come in this series, but the seed had not germinated until one weekend the following November.

Jesus taught that before a grain of wheat can bear fruit it must first fall into the ground and die. In the same way this seed of an idea sprang to life as the result of death, for during the two weeks prior to this weekend no less than six of my colleagues lost their lives as the result of gun or bomb attacks.

One of these men was Sergeant Stephen Fyfe, a close associate who had worked in the same office as myself and with whom I had occasionally teamed up on investigations. I also knew his father and uncle well.

Stephen died on 4th November 1983 at Jordanstown Polytechnic College where he was attending a police lecture. The IRA planted a bomb in the classroom, knowing that it would kill or maim many people. In the event, three officers died.

A couple of days later I attended Stephen's funeral at Railway Street Presbyterian Church, Lisburn, and there with his family, friends and other colleagues I was moved as the organist played 'Safe in the arms of Jesus', a hymn that has now become all-too-familiar because of Ulster's many funerals. I could never become too familiar with the sentiment, though, and for Stephen's sake I was glad. The terrorists could do him no harm now. That truth burned in my soul that morning, for truth it was. As the scripture says, 'We know these things are true by believing, not by seeing.'

As I stood looking at the coffin, draped with the Union Flag, and as I watched Stephen's dad blinking back the tears, I felt this faith stir within me. It was, I believe, an important moment in the birth of this project. 'Go forward with the book,' God seemed to be saying to me. 'Move out in faith.'

This was echoed through the pages of the 'Golden Grain' diary I used each day. Opening it up to enter an engagement for the following month, I read these words: 'Let us move on and step out boldly. There are things that God gives us to do without any light, but those who know the way to God can find their way in the dark.'

We were passing through dark times all right – had been for many years – but at that point I didn't think the darkness of the troubles could get any deeper. How wrong I was! Before I could even begin making notes for this book we were to see the men of violence stoop to an all-time low.

At our church it was the annual Missionary Weekend. Earlier in the day we'd benefited from the ministry of our guest speaker, Dr Peter Cotterell, and now, as we headed out to church on the Sunday evening, we were looking forward to hearing him speak on evangelism – the missionary role of the church in the local community. We couldn't have known it then, but before Sunday was through the concept of 'the local church' was to be on the lips of a stunned nation.

I first became aware that something was up about half way through the service. Outside, beyond the church windows, the familiar blue lights could be seen flashing by, and somewhere in the distance a siren was wailing. This was nothing new; because of the location of our church we were used to hearing the sound of emergency or security vehicles speeding past, so we thought little of it and set our minds to absorbing our speaker's message. Personally, I was encouraged by Dr Cotterell's remarks and felt enthusiastic about the two days I'd planned to have off that week in order to begin the initial planning of this book. But soon my enthusiasm was to evaporate. At least for a while.

'Dad, there are policemen standing guard outside,' Clive told me as I reached the back of the church.

'What are they there for?' asked Keri. 'They've got rifles and things.'

'I've no idea,' I told them. 'Probably just an exercise.'

But it was no such thing, and as it turned out our church wasn't the only one in the area to receive a police guard that night. When we arrived home and switched on the TV news we realised why. In a horrifying display of violence that almost defied belief, terrorists had burst into a small country church in the farming village of Darkley and opened fire on the congregation. At the time the worshippers were standing, singing a hymn. The gunmen, giving no thought to women or children, sprayed the congregation with bullets, killing three and wounding seven. It was an act of murder that shook the nation rigid, and even, it is said, appalled leaders of the terrorist groupings, all of whom denied responsibility by their men. Eventually it was established that the attack had been carried out by renegade members of the INLA (Irish National Liberation Army), but to the sickened peoples of Northern Ireland, Protestants and Catholics alike, the identity of the group was unimportant; as a people we were in shock. With so much violence over the years, so much cold-blooded murder, the man in the street had perhaps begun to believe that he had grown accustomed to it all and that he could no longer know that stomach-churning revulsion at an act of murder. Darkley had proved him painfully wrong.

As I sat down at the typewriter the following morning I too felt that pain. More than that, I was confused. In my

21

spirit I was still smarting from the death of Stephen Fyfe and my other RUC colleagues – and now this.

Why did God allow such things to happen? Over years of investigating murders in Northern Ireland I have asked that question many times. *Why?* Oh, I knew the pat answer: that God has given man a free will and that those gunmen had freely chosen to kill. And I knew, too, that in the scheme of things my God would not allow a trusting man or woman to die before his or her time. But answers did not necessarily bring understanding.

I thought again of those words from the diary: 'There are things God gives us to do without any light, but those who know the way to God can find their way in the dark.' It looked like that was as close to understanding as I would ever get. I turned to the typewriter . . .

But an hour or so later I was still staring at a blank sheet of paper.

Lord, it's hard to write in the dark . . .

By ten o'clock, still blocked, I decided to break off for a coffee. Lily was out and the kids were at school, so I took my drink into the lounge to listen to a record. Instinctively, I reached for one of my favourite albums – a collection of Marijohn Wilkin's songs – and sat back to let those familiar sounds sooth a policeman's troubled mind. But comfort wasn't the only thing I was to derive from Marijohn's music that morning. Many times I have felt as though God himself was speaking to me through this lady's songs, and that day he did it again. The song was entitled 'Let Your Faith Take You Places', and the lyrics ran like this:

If something's happening in your life that you don't
    understand,
Consider the enormity of God's unfolding plan;
Don't try to analyse it with words like Why or How –
Someday you'll know the answer, though you can't
    find it now.

Let your faith take you places your mind can't figure
  out;
There's no way in this world to know what God's
  about.
Be grateful for your blessings, pray when you're in
  doubt,
And let your faith take you places your mind can't
  figure out.

The message was so powerful that I had to play that
track again, and when it was through I went back to the
typewriter with a prayer of thanks and a clear head. I
didn't have any answers for those murders, nor for the
years of bloodshed, but I was sure of one thing: that
somewhere in the midst of all the suffering, our God was
at work. And that he was sovereign. I couldn't expect to
comprehend his purposes, I knew, but I could trust him.
That was the way forward with the book.

As I thought about these things – suffering, darkness,
faith – I saw a principle begin to emerge: that if the hand
of God was to be found anywhere, it was in the shadow of
suffering. I had learned this long ago, not through police
work, but through being around the very special person
who was my mother.

It all seems so long ago now – almost as though it
happened to someone else in another world – and yet at
times, when I need them, the memories burn bright and
clear.

In all the nineteen years I spent at home in our little
terraced house in Craigwell Avenue, Portadown, I can
count on one hand the number of times I remember
Mum going out. She suffered severely from rheumatoid
arthritis, a wickedly crippling condition that restricted
her movements and brought her much pain from the
time that I was a young boy onward. This meant that we
all had to do what we could to help. Shopping, for
example, was a shared effort by Dad, Leah and myself.
We were fortunate, of course, that Dad was a butcher

and so always had the makings of a fine meal at his fingertips, and that the breadman and grocer called regularly. But there were always other things we needed, and for these Leah and I used to run to Stevenson's, our favourite corner shop. 'And how's Mother today?' Mrs Stevenson frequently would ask, and frequently we would say, 'Oh, about the same.'

We lived with pain. To a degree, our lives were ordered around it. Even as a boy of ten I had to help Dad get Mum upstairs and into bed at night, and what an ordeal that was. Then, in the dark hours, I would sometimes lie awake in my bed listening to Mum crying with the pain. I can hear her now; she would cry and cry.

As I say, she rarely left the house, and even the one outing which is the most vivid to me was marred by that unrelenting illness. It was one of those magic occasions for children when fantasy becomes reality. Roy Rogers, the star of all those great cowboy films, was appearing *in person* at the Belfast Opera House, along with his amazing horse, Trigger. Dad's boss, always a kind and caring man, had arranged to take us all in his car, and no one can imagine the excitement Leah and I felt as we set off. Roy Rogers!

Almost inevitably, though, our journey was interrupted by Mum's suffering; the car had to be stopped because she was feeling sick.

In my own childish way I used to pray that Mum would get well – that the sickness would go away – and at times I would be so upset by listening to her sobs in our shared room that I would cry myself to sleep.

But nothing changed. Except, perhaps, that she got worse. Looking back at those years, and perhaps now being more able to appreciate just how wearing must have been the daily persistence of her suffering, I find it remarkable that never once did I hear my mother complain. Instead she chose to bear her burden with a smile and a lightness that made our home a happy one; a good place to be. For throughout the raging storm of her suffering, Mum possessed a personal inner peace that sustained her – and us – throughout those long years. It was a peace, I now realise, that came through her faith. If she were here today, I'm sure she would explain it as she explained so many things, by pointing me to the pages of her much-loved old Bible.

'See here, Ben,' she would say, 'just read this for yourself.' And somehow I think she would be showing me that verse in Philippians: 'And the peace of God, which passeth all understanding, shall keep your hearts and minds through Christ Jesus.' That peace, which I have now experienced for myself, was what kept her going, and what kept her so cheerful.

In addition to a smile Mum often had a tune on her lips. She loved music – something else she passed on to me – and often Leah and I would burst through the front door to find her quietly singing to herself as she laboured painfully at some chore.

I remember one song that she was particularly fond of. It was called 'Brighten the Corner Where You Are', and it ran like this:

Do not wait until some deed of greatness you may do;
Do not wait to shed your light afar.
To the many duties ever near you now be true –
Brighten the corner where you are.

Brighten the corner where you are;
Brighten the corner where you are.
Someone far from harbour you may guide across the
    bar;
Brighten the corner where you are.

I understand why that song appealed to Mum, apart from the catchy tune. The words were most relevant to her situation because in a very real sense she was in a corner, and that was the only place she *could* brighten. She did it gladly and consistently, letting the light of her faith shine through the darkness of her personal circumstances, and proving to those of us who had to watch her suffer that there is a joy which not even years of pain can destroy.

After I committed my own life to Christ – partly the result of my mother's godly influence upon my young life – I prayed even harder that this disease that had gripped her would go away, and I was hopeful that God would answer. He did, but it seems to me that he said 'no'. I couldn't understand it then, of course, but now I accept it, just as the Apostle Paul had finally accepted the same answer after God had consistently declined to remove what Paul called his 'thorn in the flesh' (traditionally thought to be an affliction of the eyes). God's answer then was, 'No – my grace is sufficient for you.' Or, as my Living Bible puts it, 'No. But I am with you; that is all you need. My power shows up best in weak people.'

Certainly that was true in Mum's case, and certainly those years of living in the same house with her taught me, as I have said, that if the hand of God is to be found anywhere, it is in the shadow of suffering.

In the broader scheme of things, I am inclined to think that those years were my training ground for having to live with another type of suffering – that which I see around me day after day as I go about my work as a member of the security forces in Northern Ireland. Certainly these present circumstances, like Mum's, have caused me many times to pray a similar prayer: that God will take away the sickness that has gripped our land – the sickness of terrorism.

I am hopeful that he will do just that, but at the same time I know that sometimes we can pray all we want and still be told, 'No – my grace is sufficient for you.'

If that is the answer we receive – and as I write I see no indication that the troubles might at last be coming to an end – then I am willing to trust my God to carry me through. He is strong enough, and I am weak enough, to make a good team. And even if he declines to give me any light on why this murder or that sickness should be allowed, I shall at least know that I will not be alone as I press on through the darkness. Just as he promised: 'I am with you; that is all you need.'

And if, as may well happen, the going gets tougher still, I know that *by faith* I can raise my sights to glimpse my destination – that other city, the beautiful City of God, already being enjoyed by those who have gone on before.

3: The choice

It was a Tuesday morning and the traffic was flowing well as I drove down into the centre of Belfast. Normally my journey into the city is punctuated with bottle-neck jams and other delays, but today I was much earlier than usual and the roads were clear.

I was thankful; I was headed for a special appointment – a Christian businessmen's breakfast – and as the organisers had kindly invited me to attend as guest speaker I didn't want to be late.

I needn't have worried; at 7.40, with plenty of time to spare, I swung the car into the Europa Hotel car park. Then I was away across the road to the breakfast venue, the popular Skandia Restaurant, where various early-bird businessmen were already arriving.

At eight o'clock, with about thirty present, we settled to a grand 'Ulster Fry' breakfast – not a calorie counter in sight! – and then our host, Ronnie Irvine, was giving a few words of introduction before handing over to the speaker.

Glancing at the clock, for each of us had our own business to attend to before long, I got to my feet and launched away. My theme was 'Christ and Crime', and for twenty minutes or so I shared something of the part my faith plays in my work as a member of the RUC's Criminal Investigation Department, and there was still time left at the end for a few questions from the floor. When finally I sat down again it was with the hope that something of what I'd had to say would be meaningful to at least some of those present.

For me, however, the most memorable moment came after the meeting had been formally closed and the tables were being cleared. It was then that I got talking with one of the businessmen – I'll call him Harry – and it was through him, as a result of his son's death, that I was to hear some helpful words.

Harry's son John was twenty-three years of age when he died. A young businessman, he was doing well in his profession and was said to have a bright future ahead of him. But all promise was dashed one afternoon after a business call in West Belfast. As he was leaving a client's premises a motor vehicle drew alongside him, the driver produced a gun, and moments later John lay dead on the pavement.

The family's grief was accentuated by the fact that a terrorist group, in claiming responsibility, acknowledged that they'd made a mistake; that they'd shot the wrong man. John had died for nothing.

'I've been through some black moments since then,' Harry told me. 'Some dark and deep depressions. And without Christ I don't think I'd have coped.'

He went on to tell me something I've heard all too often in the course of my work – that losing a loved one to the gunmen can give rise to a deep-seated hatred that in turn can lead to thoughts of retaliation and even suicide.

'But that's no use, you see,' Harry went on, his eyes faintly moist, 'for that way you only do the terrorists' work for them; that's just adding coal to their fire.' He shook his head. 'No, it's bad enough to lose what's dearest to you, but if you allow hatred and bitterness to take root you'll lose yourself, too. I know – I came close.'

Harry then went on to express his appreciation of what I was seeking to do in spreading the message of Christ through my books and records and other means. 'But there's one thing that needs emphasising,' he told me. 'One thing that those who've suffered like myself need to hear, and it's this: Be careful that your experience of evil does not destroy you. For it surely will, if you let it.'

Those words were to stick. A little later, as I went for the car and moved out into the traffic again – the real bottle-neck stuff this time – I found myself mentally repeating and storing them.

Be careful that your experience of evil does not destroy you.

In these profound terms Harry had highlighted the real agony that is Ulster today, for terrorism, despite all the physical violence, is actually *a war of the mind*. The real issue facing us, I reminded myself, was not what the terrorists achieved with their bullets and their bombs, but how we *reacted* to such atrocities.

There was a choice to be made – a choice that at some time or other was likely to touch every living soul in Northern Ireland – and the way we chose to go would determine whether or not the terrorists achieved their goal. If, like so many, we chose bitterness, self-pity, vengeance, the terrorists would be well pleased. But if, like Harry, we refused to be sucked into the dark whirlpool of unforgiveness, the enemy would be robbed of all victory.

Over the years I've seen many grief-stricken families face that choice, and sadly I've known many to take the easier, downhill route. In the course of my work I've heard more than one widow pour out venom towards both God and the assassin as she vented her frustration and bitterness; and months later I've heard those same women explain how such an unforgiving spirit, coupled with a prayer-vengeance against the evildoer, turned out to be the first steps on the road to both mental and physical breakdown. On their own admission, these women had allowed their experience of evil to destroy them.

Likewise, I've had to interview men – perhaps bereaved fathers, sons or brothers – who allowed seeds of vengeance to take root and shortly found themselves slithering down the slippery slope into the ranks of the illegal paramilitaries. They too, in allowing themselves to take up the gun, and seeking to take the law into their own hands, had discovered to their cost and shame that their experience of evil had destroyed them.

Thankfully, though, there were also those who had chosen the tougher, uphill path of peace. *These*, not the bitter gunmen, were the brave ones, for it takes far more courage to battle on against the heartache day after day than it does to squeeze a trigger.

I'd had occasion to meet many such courageous people – people I have come to number among the real heroes of Northern Ireland – and some of them had become part of my own life and had been written about in my earlier books. Always I am amazed at how such people cope in their daunting circumstances (for I never kid myself that to forgive is easy), but more often than not I discover that the reason their experience of evil has not destroyed them is because in their weakness they have reached out to the source and giver of perfect strength, the Lord Jesus Christ.

As I headed across town, making for my base on the east side of the city, some of these 'heroes' came to mind. One was Avril Cummings, whose husband Neville – my partner for five years – had died in an IRA booby-trap explosion. Avril was left with three children to raise and she had found it very difficult to accept Neville's death, as well she might.

Like every other woman widowed by the terrorists, Avril had had to face 'the choice'. But those who know her will tell you that there's no doubt about the way she has chosen to go, and how she has found the strength to travel that road. How could anyone doubt when they read these words from a letter Avril sent to me recently when I was going through my own difficulties:

'Don't be discouraged,' she wrote, 'for the Lord is good and he doesn't let anything happen that we cannot bear with his help. Maybe we won't know now, but there is a purpose in everything. Hold fast unto him, for there is nothing or no one who can be compared with him.'

As I drove on, my mind went to Florence Cobb, the police widow who not only forgave her husband's killer but also wrote to him to express that forgiveness. Her moving testimony to God's peace and power in the human heart was broadcast far and wide through the media and touched many lives throughout the world. But Florence too had her battle; she too had faced the choice.

'I shed many, many tears over Harold's death,' she told me, 'and I went through all the dark tunnels of grief – loneliness, depression, self-pity – but you destroy yourself if you allow those feelings to get hold of you.

'The children too had their time of grief. Alan was 15, Ivan 13 and Pauline six, and they all loved their daddy very much. But the Lord sustained us all and brought us out of it without bitterness. When I wrote to Harold's assassin it was with the children's approval.'

As I drove up through My Lady's Road I thought of Jennie Davidson, another RUC widow whose husband Gerald died when IRA snipers opened fire on a police Land-Rover in which he was travelling. Like Avril and Florence, Jennie too had been left with children to raise, and there was no hatred. Yet there was still a choice to be made.

'I couldn't forgive – not at first,' Jennie told me. 'It took eighteen months. After that I began to realise just how much these people are victims of circumstance, and that "there but for the grace of God go I". Understanding isn't enough, though; it's only a beginning. We have to tell the terrorists that God loves them – that *we* love them – and that with God's help they can change. They need to know that, and if it comes down to me . . . yes, I'll tell Gerald's murderers that Jesus loves them.'

Another name that came to mind that morning was Thomas Maxwell, a sprightly 79-year-old whose house I'd called at following the murder of his son Norman. At Tennent Street Police Station, where Mr Maxwell helped us with our inquiries, he had told me through his tears that neither he nor his family sought vengeance for Norman's death. Clearly there was no trace of bitterness in this fine old gentleman's heart. 'I'm a Christian, you see,' he explained, 'and Norman's death doesn't alter the fact that God loves me, or that I love him.' And with moving compassion he added: 'No, we seek no vengeance. Rather we would hope that the Spirit of God would work in the hearts of those responsible and that they would be saved for all eternity.'

As I turned into the police station yard, one more name surfaced from the memories of so many whose positive response to their hurts had been such an encouragement in my own life. This time I could not put a face to the name, for it belonged to a soldier whom I'd never met, but whose letters had inspired me just the same. This soldier, a Coldstream Guardsman, had been blown up by a 100-lb bomb whilst serving in Crossmaglen, down in the 'bandit country' of Armagh. During his stay in hospital he had read *Hope in 'Bomb City'* and felt moved to write to me.

'I found the book helped me not to accept the bomber's reason,' he wrote, 'but to forgive an unknown terrorist, and also to thank God for a miraculous escape from what should have been certain death.

'Whilst never paying more than lip service to religion, my recent convalescence has given me opportunity to ponder on the nature of God . . . and feel myself drawn nearer to him.

'Many thanks for hope, and indeed a measure of salvation.'

The books have brought many letters over the years and I try to reply to each one. When I posted off my acknowledgement to this guardsman I enclosed a copy of *Love in 'Bomb City'*, seeking to encourage him further in his thoughts towards God.

Some weeks later, after he'd returned to the mainland, the soldier wrote again, and I was delighted to read that he now felt able 'to call you a fellow Christian'. What struck me most about his letter, though, was his closing line: 'Best wishes, and stay in his love and peace.'

It seemed to me that in these few words this man had captured what is surely the secret of forgiveness and the key to ensuring 'that your experience of evil does not destroy you'. These were the discoveries that Avril, Florence, Jennie and so many others had made. There was nothing superhuman about such people; they were not blessed in some special way with the strength of character which enabled them to respond without hatred or malice to what the terrorists had done. The fact that they had been able to ride the storm of grief and to forgive those who had hurt them was no credit to themselves. All they had done was to choose God's way instead of the way of the human heart. Realising their own inability to handle the situation, they had looked beyond themselves to their loving heavenly Father. Rather than sinking into despair, they had cried to the Lord for help. And he – he alone – had enabled them to 'stay in his love and peace'.

I too had made this discovery, for over the years I'd had good cause to seek the Lord's help, and on occasions to make that critical choice. When Neville Cummings died, for example, I went through a period of grief for a fine partner and friend, and occasionally dark thoughts of vengeance reared their ugly head in my own mind.

Likewise, when terrorists tried to hijack my wife's car, putting both Lily and Clive at risk, my first reaction was not a Christian one. I knew that through my various contacts I would be able to discover who those men were and where to find them, and when I began phoning around for information it was with every intention of doing them harm.

Thankfully, Lily's commonsense and our mutual faith prevailed, and by the time we tucked Clive into bed that night we had forgiven those men and were able to pray that they would find God's peace.

There had been other times, too, when a choice had to be made – such as when I narrowly escaped death as a terrorist bomb exploded only eight feet from where I stood. Only because a concrete-mixer lorry passed between myself and the bomb at the moment of detonation am I still here to tell the tale.

Looking back on these and other trials – particularly the many occasions when I've been faced with the bloody remains of police colleagues slaughtered by the various terrorist groups – I'm able to appreciate just what enormous strength I've derived through my faith in Jesus Christ. And if, as Harry counselled, I've been able to avoid letting my experience of evil destroy me, it's largely due to the presence of God's Spirit within . . . and the fact that, when it's come to the crunch, I've somehow managed – even if it's after a struggle – to 'stay in his love and peace'.

As I parked the car and headed into the office that morning my thoughts went finally to another family that was facing the choice and experiencing God's peace – police widow May Brown and her three daughters. I thought of them because that evening I was to sing at a church concert and I understood that May and two of the girls would be there.

For this family the grief was still very real, for it had been only two months since the husband and father, Sergeant Eric Brown, had died. I had met Eric only once, and it's an occasion I'm not likely to forget!

4: Only a prayer away

Eric Brown and I were brought together through our mutual membership of the Christian Police Association, a body which had provided many opportunities for Christian fellowship and teaching throughout the years of our careers, and which had now arranged a weekend conference in Leicester. About twenty-five members of the Northern Ireland CPA were booked to attend, among them Eric and myself. We met on our way to that conference aboard the Larne–Stranraer ferry, in the cafeteria. Lily and I, along with other officers and their wives, had retreated there to escape the fresh Irish Sea winds blowing on deck, and to take a snack. It was there at the tables that we first experienced Eric's great sense of fun.

He was, without doubt, a born entertainer – the life of any party – and if he wasn't joking about the sausage rolls –'Are yours cardboard or rubber?' – it was the 'poorer' members of the party, with their packed lunches, who came in for some of Eric's wit.

Sitting opposite him, I thought it only a matter of time before he directed his humour at me, and sure enough he had quite a few things to say about the fact that we happened to be wearing the same shoes – 'Blue Barkers'. 'Affluent taste for a couple of bobbies, eh?' he grinned. 'They must be paying us too much!'

I made some crack about overtime – but I didn't tell him that *my* pair of 'expensive' shoes happened to be seconds. He would have made a joke of that, too!

Eric kept us laughing for quite a while that afternoon, not only on the ferry but on the coach, too, as it bore us on the long journey from Stranraer to Leicester. And once at our destination Eric's cheerful chatter quickly won him even more friends.

Yes, Eric Brown was quite a comic – but he was no fool. There was another, equally impressive side to this man: his faith was just as lively as his sense of fun, and when in conversation with individuals over the weekend, or as he spoke from the platform on the theme of 'The Christian Policeman', he had a way of communicating his relationship with Jesus Christ that was instantly appealing and . . . yes, inspiring.

No one who met Eric that weekend was likely to forget him in a hurry, and when, on the Monday morning, our little group returned to Larne and we went our separate ways, there were many of us who felt we'd made a good friend. Personally, I was looking forward to the next time we would meet.

But that was not to be. On a cold, brisk Thursday morning – the first in 1983 – Eric was on mobile patrol with two colleagues when they stopped in the seaside village of Rostrevor, County Down, to investigate a suspicious-looking car parked outside the post office. It was eleven o'clock in the morning and the car contained two men.

While Eric and full-time reservist Brian Quinn remained in their unmarked police car, another officer approached the men. Immediately, they turned with guns in their hands and opened fire. In the hail of bullets, the advancing officer was wounded. Eric and Brian Quinn died instantly, still inside their car.

It is believed that the police officers had happened upon terrorists who were about to hold up the post office. Their guns were already primed.

Things happen so suddenly in Northern Ireland. In a single moment – all the time it takes to squeeze a trigger – our plans can be changed. That week I'd been looking forward to a free Saturday when I'd be able to tackle a few jobs around the house. Now I would be going to a funeral.

The historic town of Moira, the Browns' home, came to a standstill that afternoon. Even though it was a bitterly cold day with an icy wind scything through the streets, crowds of sad-eyed locals packed the pavements and hundreds gathered to march with Eric's remains to the church. It was a witness to just how much the man was respected and loved. And to how great was our loss.

The cortège, led by the RUC band playing its all-too-familiar death march, included many of Eric's colleagues, and just to look around brought a sobering reminder of how many members of the force, and how many RUC families, had been affected by the violence of the past fourteen years.

Behind me, to my right, walked Ivan, a former colleague whose police career had abruptly ended with two IRA bullets in the brain.

Just ahead of me, and being led by another ex-officer, was Charlie, now blind as the result of a terrorist bomb.

Further ahead, but standing out from the crowd because of their height, were two brothers, Alan and Ivan, whose father, an RUC inspector, was murdered by an IRA sniper in Lurgan.

And over there . . . well, there were just too many to name; too many even to think about.

What was the point of it all? Where was the sense in so much wanton violence? And what answers could I give – even as a Christian – to May and her girls on such a day as this?

We moved on, keeping pace behind the hearse as the procession eased into the main street, and there my eyes fell upon something which was to remind me that our God was still in control; that, despite the apparent triumph of evil, the victory was Christ's.

Christmas was over, but the town's decorated tree still stood in the square, a somewhat intrusive reminder of happier days. Yet, as I looked, that tree seemed to offer a message that spoke right into the darkness of our present situation. At the top of its branches, bowing to one side in the cruel wind, hung the Christmas star. In the same way, I thought, my Saviour hung his head when on the tree of Calvary. For him too the festivities had come to an end; for him too there had come a time to bow in submission before the winds of hatred.

Yet, unlike the star, Jesus had made his own choice. He didn't *have* to die on the cross; he could have chosen to live on. His love for us, however, far outweighed his human inclination to shrink from death.

The same was true of Eric. Yes, with one last glance at the star I realised that Eric too had sought to put others before himself. Like so many of his colleagues who'd gone before him, Eric had not said 'no' to serving the community; to putting his life on the line, and eventually losing it, for the sake of his fellows.

What had Jesus said about it? 'Greater love has no man than this, that a man lay down his life for his friends.'

Eric Brown, Brian Quinn, and more than 150 other RUC officers had bravely demonstrated that love for the peoples of Northern Ireland since the present troubles had begun in 1969. Likewise, over 350 British soldiers and more than 100 members of the UDR (Ulster Defence Regiment). In addition, more than 8,000 members of the security forces had been injured, many seriously.

Perhaps some, I mused, would prefer to call it loyalty rather than love, but it amounted to the same thing: each of those men (and women) had served their country selflessly, gladly. They had not shrunk from their final call of service – the supreme sacrifice.

As we moved on, the band playing a selection of appropriate hymns, my mind went again to May and her three daughters – Michelle, 17, 13-year-old Sonje, and Andrea, 12. This was indeed a black day for them.

What, I wondered, could possibly lighten the dark times ahead?

Perhaps the key to this lay in the very moving address given in church that day by the Browns' rector, Rev. C.R.J. Rudd. Referring to May and the girls – but speaking to each one in that packed parish church – he said: 'They all have their faith properly fixed on God. Without that they could not carry on. That is what our faith is for, to enable us to climb mountains, and fight battles, and face problems. And we all have the assurance that God will never fail us. Our faith equips us even to face something like this.'

Looking from my seat in the small gallery I was able to glance down at May and her three daughters, their shoulders jerking frequently with their sobs, and I was prompted to pray that their faith would hold firm.

Over the following weeks, on the two occasions when Lily and I visited them in their home (once with police widow Jennie Davidson), I was impressed as to how my prayers, and the prayers of the many who had been remembering the Browns from day to day, were being answered. Though tears still came readily to their eyes, there was an underlying peace – a peace which I'd witnessed in the lives of other police families deprived of husband and father, and which never failed to move me. I refrained from commenting upon it, though; in fact I said very little at all on those visits, for Jennie Davidson, who'd been through the grief herself, had once given me some advice on the matter, and I'd found it to be wisdom. 'Don't talk,' she'd told me. 'Just listen. Your willingness to do that will be appreciated far more than any words.'

For a man whose job demands that he be able to talk, sometimes for hours on end, to people brought into the police interview rooms, that was quite a challenge. After a while, though, as we sat back in the Browns' comfortable lounge and listened as May shared what was on her heart, I found that I didn't want to talk anyway. And –

remarkably – once I'd given up any idea of saying something helpful, I began to *receive* from May. For much of what she said, as well as emphasising her family's faith, underlined my own. And we covered a lot of ground.

'The Scriptures are true enough when they speak of a peace that passes understanding,' May told us. 'It's quite irrational in the circumstances, but it's powerful – just as though the Lord himself is here, embracing us, supporting us. It's so real, so strong.'

Another time she said, 'Sometimes I've lain awake at night, weeping and asking why it had to happen – and wondering who was responsible. Of course I may never know, but the Lord knows those men, and with God's help we've been able to pray that they will come to know Christ. If that happened I'd somehow feel that it was all worthwhile. At the moment it just seems such a waste. But God knows best, doesn't he?'

And at one point she remarked, 'I know it's not for ever, this separation. Just a little while and we'll see Eric again. If I didn't believe that I don't think I could carry on.'

Driving home after that second visit I found my words still reluctant to leave my lips, but Lily phrased my sentiments exactly. 'Thank the Lord that death *isn't* the end, Ben. Where would people like May be without that hope.'

'Or any of us,' I said, finding my voice at last. 'Especially in this crazy part of the world. Believe me, Lily, sometimes I think it's only looking beyond this scene to those mansions above that keeps a man sane.'

'Let not your heart be troubled,' Lily responded, quoting Jesus. 'Ye believe in God, believe also in me. In my father's house are many mansions.'

I let the text flow on in my mind: 'If it were not so, I would have told you. I go to prepare a place for you. And if I go and prepare a place for you, I will come again, and receive you unto myself; that where I am, there ye may be also.'

42

As we headed up out of Moira and on to the motorway, I thought how much that promise would mean to May and the girls in the coming days. As Lily had said, thank God that death *isn't* the end: that, for the Christian, it is but a new beginning; and that, in time, all who believe will be reunited with those who have gone on before. That was comfort indeed.

The thought was to be continued a few weeks later, one evening in March – the day I met Harry at the businessmen's breakfast. Returning home from the office that afternoon there was only time for a quick tea and a chat with the family before Lily and I headed out in the car for Raffrey Presbyterian Church, deep in the County Down farming country. That was where I was to sing, at the concert which May would be attending. It had been organised to help raise funds for the church's Girl's Brigade company, and the invitation, gladly accepted, had come through one of the Raffrey GB officers who worked in the office at Castlereagh Police Station. Having had the date marked in my diary for some weeks, we were now on our way. Lily was coming with me to control the backing tapes (the music tracks from my recordings) and together we appreciated the opportunity to renew acquaintances with many old friends, not least the church's minister and his wife, Trevor and Dorothy Anderson.

I was also glad of the chance to meet up again with organist Jim Young. Back in my 'A' Division days, when I was stationed at Donegall Pass, I often called into Jim's Belfast music shop and we had many a good conversation, not to mention a good laugh. Tonight some of the memories would be stirred as Jim and I shared the platform. We weren't to be alone. Also due to take part were the Baillies Mill Accordian Band and a harmony singing group, The Gospelaires.

At 7.15, as Lily and I pressed into the already crowded church and made towards the front, I was glad for the GB's sake that all the tickets had been sold. By the time the accordian band had struck up its first number it was 'standing room only'.

The band set the tone for the evening – relaxed with plenty of audience participation – and when it was my turn to get up and sing I decided to continue the mood with a hymn that I thought many would know: 'How Great Thou Art'. It was obviously a popular choice, but I'd barely got into the song when suddenly I heard a small cry. Glancing down, I saw young Andrea Brown move across to be comforted by her mum, and it occurrred to me that I might be singing one of Eric's favourite hymns. At least, the song seemed to have revived memories for Andrea and had prompted tears. As I sang on, unsure as to whether that was the right thing to do, the weeping spread to Sonje, to May, and, before long, to many of those seated around them. Diffidently, I carried on, and by the time I was through it seemed the entire audience was sharing something of the grief of this family. As the last notes of the music died away, every head in the place bowed in spontaneous prayer.

When the moment had passed I sent up a prayer for myself: *Lord, what should I do?* The answer came immediately. Looking across at the tearful family, I said, 'May, I have to sing on.'

May nodded, smiling bravely, and so I continued, hoping that my choice of songs would not be too painful for these hurting hearts. When it came to my last piece I chose one of my favourites: 'Only a Prayer Away'. It's a song I've sung many times, but on this occasion the words took on a fresh meaning as I looked at young Andrea and Sonje. Maybe, I thought, this is just for them – a reminder that their dad was with the Lord Jesus, who was just a prayer away. I hoped it was. My heart went out to these two girls – not a lot younger than my own daughter Keri – and perhaps the father in me wanted to reassure them.

But we had to move on. Soon my time was up, someone else was taking the stage, and I was slipping into the pew alongside Lily and the tape machine.

The concert came to a close at around 9.20, and then it was time for the very appealing supper the church had laid on. Well able to face a sandwich or three, I took my place in the queue along with everyone else, and as we got munching and chatting I quite forgot about the Brown girls. But they hadn't forgotten me. Half an hour later, thinking I really couldn't manage another crumb, young Andrea and Sonje – their tears long forgotten – came across and offered me one of their sweets – cinammon lozenges. Well, how could I refuse?

'Very nice,' I remarked, getting my tongue around this new taste.

'Do you like them?' asked Sonje.

'I do.'

'Here then – you can have the packet.'

Such generosity from a wee girl. 'Are you sure?'

'Aye – I don't like them, anyway.'

I laughed and slipped the sweets into my pocket. 'Thank you, girls.' I was touched by this little act of generosity – even if Sonje *didn't* like the taste! – and I found myself wanting to reciprocate the gesture. But what could I possibly give them?

A moment later, though, I realised that the sweets were in exchange for what I'd already given them.

'Would you do us a favour?' asked Andrea. 'Would you let us have the words of that song – "Only a Prayer Away"?'

5: The one that got away

It was going to be a long night. Sitting opposite me in interview room A7 at Castlereagh Police Station was a young man brought in for questioning in connection with a murder in East Belfast. It was a particularly vicious crime – a sectarian murder – and it was obvious that the person facing me across the table was not going to co-operate. Though there was a certain amount of evidence which pointed to his involvement in the crime, it was all circumstantial, and this youngster – I'll call him Donald – knew it.

As far as obstructing the police in the course of their inquiries, Donald had been well versed. He made good use of the individual's right to remain silent while being questioned, and when he did speak it was to hurl some piece of abuse at me. That didn't worry me, of course – it comes with the job – but as a Christian policeman coming into contact with people caught up in the violence of the land we share, my concern is on two levels.

First and foremost my responsibility is to seek to reach the truth in any set of circumstances I'm called to investigate, and, where appropriate, to see that charges are preferred and justice done.

On another level is my concern for the person himself. I believe that anyone who gets involved in crime, whether terrorism or otherwise, needs help, and over the years I have sought to reach out a hand of friendship to many of the people I have had cause to interview. I'm not saying I have all the answers, but I do believe that when a man is down it is my responsibility as a Christian to offer him a lift up. The opportunity for such action does not always present itself, of course; some of the hard-bitten characters I've questioned would spit on your hand if you offered it to them. However, years of dealing with individuals have also shown me that these people are in the minority; that, by and large, most offenders fall into crime as the result of being trapped by their circumstances, and that, deep down, they welcome the offer of a hand up.

But not Donald. I tried everything I knew to reach that young man, but he would not respond either to my official inquiries or to my personal approach as a fellow human being seeking to help. He did not want my help and told me what I could do with it.

There is always a reason for such hostility. A young man is the product of his surroundings – a reflection of the attitudes which influenced his youth – and sometimes it is possible to tune in to a person's thought-waves by opening a few doors in his past. Which is how I came to be asking Donald about his family, especially his father. Significantly, this was about the only time the lad showed any sign of beginning to open up.

'You can forget about him,' Donald snapped. 'He never cared about me. He wouldn't even give me the time o' day, so don't go talking to him about me. He won't help you. He never helped *me* before . . .'

As I said, it was going to be a long night. Time can drag when you have to sit questioning someone for hour after hour, knowing all the time that you're not going to get anywhere, and by eleven o'clock I decided I'd had enough. Donald was taken down to the cells for the night and I headed home, thankful that tomorrow was a day off.

I'd promised to take Clive fishing – or perhaps it was the other way round, for the only fish I've ever caught were battered and wrapped in newspaper – but at least it would mean a trip to the coast.

When I surfaced from my lie-in the following morning Clive was all packed and rearing to go. 'I've been thinking, Dad – maybe we could go to Donaghadee instead of the River Bann. Is that too far?'

'No, it's only twenty miles or so, son. Has Mummy packed us a picnic, or what?'

Lily put her head round the kitchen door. 'You've sandwiches and a flask of soup, and there are a few biscuits and things. Good afternoon, Ben!'

'Good morning, Lily. Clive, make sure we've a good supply of chocolate. Fishing's hungry work.'

'And what would *you* know about it?' came Lily's laughing voice.

'Listen,' I replied, heading for the bathroom, 'the last time I went for cod and chips I had to wait for hours!'

We set out at around two o'clock with the promise of a good afternoon's relaxation ahead of us. Clive was to fish and I was to watch – a very satisfactory arrangement, I thought, until Clive suggested I might be helpful and bait his hooks for him.

'Now wait a minute, son . . .' The idea of putting a worm on a hook makes *me* squirm, never mind the worm!

Thankfully, both the worms and I were to be reprieved! As we motored over the Carryduff hills and on towards Newtownards, Clive remembered a little fish shop in the main street. 'We can get some fresh bait there, Dad.'

But as we parked the car and headed for the shop, *we* were the ones who got hooked! Wafting from the open doorway came the enticing smell of potted herring – a fishy little sideline on the shop's normal trade.

'Fancy some of that, Clive?' Clive never refuses food, and it did look good.

'We'll have six of those, please.' (Well, they were only *small* pots!)

'And will there be anything else?'

'We'd like some bait,' Clive piped up.

The man smiled. 'What are you after?'

There followed a brief technical discussion about the subtleties of sea and fresh water fishing, and I was glad that no one asked my opinion. One fish looks much like another to me, so I let the experts get on with it.

Suitably equipped, and well weighed down with potted herring, we returned to the car and continued on to the coast, arriving at around 4.30. So far everything was going to plan. But one look along the shoreline and – wait a minute! Don't you need water for fishing?

'Quick, Clive,' I laughed, 'call the police. Someone's stolen the sea!'

'Oh, no!' he groaned. 'I forgot about the tides. It could be hours before it comes in again.'

'Well, let's go and catch some potted herring while we're waiting,' I suggested. 'I don't know about you, but I'm ready for something to eat.'

We decided to take the picnic across to the nearby park, and on the way Clive spotted what appeared to be the answer to our dilemma. It was a notice down by the harbour.

'Hey, Dad, look at that – "Deep Sea Fishing Trip – Boat Leaves 6.30 pm." Could we go – *please*?'

Well, it seemed a reasonable enough request – and Clive was that keen.

'All right, son. But we're going to have a long wait.'

With a couple of hours to kill we took our time over the picnic. First to go was the soup and the potted herring, followed by the sandwiches and some wee buns. 'Enough to feed a ploughman,' I joked, 'never mind a fisherman!' Indeed it was a good spread Lily had provided and we were both quite full by the time we set off to explore the park and otherwise pass the time.

Eventually, though, the hour of our expedition drew near and we ambled back down to the harbour where the fishing boat lay gently riding the swell of the fresh tide.

'They're biting well today,' an old timer told us as we boarded the boat and were each handed a line with several hooks attached.

'Aye,' said another – and by the banter that went on between the crew and their other clients it certainly sounded as though the Irish Sea was about to lose some of its prize fish.

As for me, I wasn't too sure what to do about the fishing tackle that had been pressed into my hand, and I suspected that if I asked I'd get some very strange looks from the seasoned anglers aboard.

There was something else worrying me, too. Not only did I dislike the idea of putting worms on hooks, but I didn't exactly delight in the idea of taking fish *off* them. It was time for some tactical thinking. As we took our places in the prow of the boat and headed out into the deep, I turned to Clive. 'Look, son, you stay beside me and I'll give you all the fish I catch, provided you take them off the hook.'

Father and son knew each other well enough by now. 'Don't you worry,' chuckled Clive. 'I'll see you right.'

But there was one factor, I discovered, that could not be overcome by tactics of any kind: the movement of the boat. It really was rather more than I'd bargained for. Don't get me wrong – I love the sea and riding in boats, but I'm more used to the kind which has a cafeteria and a place to park my car. On this thing we seemed uncomfortably near the water!

The farther out we went, the more the little fishing boat rose and plunged with the churning waves . . . and the more I began to wish that I hadn't had such a good appetite in the park. Now those herring were getting their own back on me!

But once we reached our fishing patch and the skipper cut the engines, the deck stopped moving about so much and the experience became almost enjoyable.

I'm not sure how long we were out there, a dozen grown men and a couple of youngsters staring hopefully into the murky depths, but it's true what they say about fishermen having plenty of time to think. Personally I was contemplating our return to land and the comparative warmth and comfort of the car – a vision that increased with the stiffness of the sea breezes. But at least there was the occasional distraction of someone actually landing a fish or two. Thankfully, Clive caught a few – and, equally thankfully, I didn't!

It was approaching ten o'clock when the skipper decided that we'd had our money's worth and then we turned and headed back for shore.

At last!

But – oh, cruel fate! – we were only a few minutes from the harbour when suddenly I realised that the boat was turning on to another course.

'A distress signal,' the skipper informed us, poking his head out of his cockpit. 'We just had word on the radio. Sorry, but we'll have to answer the call.'

We set off round the coast in the gathering summer dusk with the engines going full speed and my stomach turning over again. Much more of this, I thought, and *I'll* be the one in distress. Clive, on the other hand, was lapping up every moment of this sudden new adventure. But if he had visions of playing the hero he was to be denied, for when we finally sighted the stricken vessel – a yacht now crashing against rocks off shore – we realised that others had answered the call more swiftly and already the wreck was surrounded by enough small boats to take every passenger off the QE2.

Considering his duty done, our skipper nosed the boat around once more, and this time we were to make it back to the harbour unhindered. We arrived in semi-darkness at eleven o'clock.

Never have I been so glad to set foot on dry land as I was that night, yet I still had enough left in me to see the funny side of the experience . . . until we had our own little disaster on our way through Newtownards. Our

Hillman, a normally reliable if somewhat noisy old car, chose this late hour – approaching midnight – to prove that nothing should ever be taken for granted.

Being as proficient a mechanic as I am a deep sea fisherman, I had a sneaking suspicion that we were in trouble. However, one is obliged to lift the bonnet on such occasions, if only to grumble at the engine, and having done this I suggested to Clive that we look for a phone-box. 'Otherwise Mummy's going to wonder what sort of fishermen we are!'

As it was, Lily had already given up on us and gone to bed. 'Sorry, love,' I yawned into the phone, 'but I think you'll have to come and rescue us.'

'Men!' she groaned.

It all turned out right in the end, of course. And Clive did get his fish. But best of all – for both of us – we had a day to remember!

Such experiences, when father and son are thrown together in some wee adventure, are perhaps of little importance in themselves. Yet in the broader tapestry of life – particularly from the son's point of view – I believe it is these colourful threads that are priceless in terms of weaving a past that will stand a boy in good stead for the future. It isn't so much a question of *what* father and son do together as the very fact of their togetherness. Such times, it seems to me, have much to do with the building of character – the development of attitudes, the learning of tolerance, the encouragement of humour, the nurturing of faith – and surely there is no other corner of the world where the need for fathers to raise their sons aright is more acute.

The choice is ours: children do not come to us with pre-programmed minds; God entrusts them to us as clay for the shaping. And whether or not they learn to go through life with the open hand of friendship or the clenched fist of bigotry is, to a large degree, at a father's discretion. This, I have realised, is a solemn responsibility, for God's anger will surely be against those who feed their sons the bitter poison of hatred rather than the sweet nourishment of love.

It is also a tremendous opportunity, for it has national as well as personal implications. I wonder, for example, whether anyone has ever considered that Ulster could be rid of 'the troubles' if every father spoke the language of forgiveness and peace to the children who play at his feet, and if every mother taught her bairns to make friends instead of nail-bombs. What a different world this would be, two generations from now! Oh, I can hear the derision of the hecklers clear enough. But we have to start somewhere, and where better than with the young ones?

I share this thought because I know what an impact for good my own father had on his son. It was mostly, I suppose, the companionship which meant most to me, especially during the early years. The memories I have of those times are brimming with smiles and laughter, and the magic of discovery and adventure. Always, it seems, there was something to do or somewhere to go, because *Dad* was always doing and going.

Our day usually started with the dogs. Dad was a keen racer of greyhounds and always we had two or three around the place, kept in the back yard. I loved those dogs. They weren't the fierce creatures that some people suppose them to be – not our dogs, anyway; ours were wonderfully tame and playful. Often I would tumble about with them on the ground, and sometimes I would snuggle up alongside them in their straw beds.

They were more than pets, though, and their daily exercise was more than a routine, especially as the racing season drew near. Each morning – up with the lark for Dad had to be at work at eight – we headed out into pale sunlight or fragile mist, treading the pavements with the dogs straining at their leads. Out of Craigwell Avenue, over the old railway bridge into Charles Street, then right into Atkinsons Lane. Here we released the dogs and let them run ahead, bounding off into the dew-wet fields like excited children.

This was the pattern for many a spring or summer morning, yet there was always a freshness about the whole routine, as though each time was the first. Once, though, I thought such a 'first time' would also be our last. Rounding a bend on a country lane, Dad and I came face to face with an enormous bull. It was just standing there in the middle of the road, as though it had been waiting for us. I was about six years old at the time, and this great beast had me shaking at the knees. I knew what to do, though, and quickly slipped in behind Dad's legs, positioning myself so as to be protected but still able to see what was going to happen. To this day I am amazed at what took place. With a dog-leash in one hand, Dad marched up to that old bull and punched it firmly on the nose. To my astonishment – not to mention my relief – the animal slowly turned and walked away.

Dad had always been something of a hero to me, but that day he was Superman. I just couldn't wait to tell the other kids in the street.

Our evening session with the dogs was usually longer and often favoured with a few goodies from McCann's sweet shop. These I munched or sucked as we trod the familiar route to Selsion Moss, an ideal place to hand-gallop the dogs because it had a good turf ramp about two hundred yards long. I would stand at one end, holding on to the dogs, while Dad went to the other. Then he would whistle and I'd release the greyhounds and watch them sprint the length of that ramper. It was always a sight to see because a small boy wondered how anything could move so fast, and Dad said you had to be careful that they didn't strike you at the end of the run for it had been known for such an impact to break a man's leg.

Weekends meant more time with Dad, particularly as Mum's illness progressed, and again it was in the simple things that I found pleasure. Depending on the season, Saturday afternoons would see us sometimes at Dungannon Stadium to race the greyhounds and sometimes at Shamrock Park for the football. The latter was a must when our own Portadown football team was playing, and on these occasions Dad and I would leave home at around 2.15 to walk the short distance to the ground. This journey was inevitably broken by another visit to Stevenson's corner shop, usually for two ounces of anniseed balls which kept a small boy sucking for the duration of the game.

On the way there we would have to pass the buses parked on the Brownstown Road, and I would always make a point of counting the green Ulster Transport Authority buses that were lined up nose to tail.

'Forty-one buses there, Dad.'

'Is that right, son? That must mean there will be forty-one goals scored today.'

Dad was always saying funny things like that. He liked to keep the conversation light and was always amusing me with tall tales about one thing or another, like building aeroplanes out of orange-boxes, or jumping over the River Bann!

It was all good fun as we made our way to Shamrock Park, and then there was the excitement of the game itself, watched by one small spectator from the lofty perch of the perimeter wall.

On such afternoons we returned home around five o'clock to find a welcome hot meal awaiting us, then after clearing the things away Dad would take Leah and me off to a local cinema (we had a choice of three) for excitement of a very different kind, like a Roy Rogers or Gene Autrey film.

And then there were Sundays. The mornings always followed the same pattern. Dad stayed at home to help around the house and Mum saw us off to Sunday School with the Jeffers boys who lived across the road and Bobby McNally whom we called for on the way.

After lunch, especially on bright summer Sundays, Dad would put a cushion on the crossbar of his bike and set me on it to cycle the eight miles or so to the Bann Foot, in the heart of the country where Dad spent his own childhood. The reason for the journey, more often than not, was to call upon Willie Matchett, one of Dad's boyhood chums who still lived in the area. Mr Matchett was a boat-builder and often he would take us down to nearby Lough Neagh where we would ride the waters in his motor-boat to the shores of Connie Island.

Such a treat was sheer magic to a small boy, of course, and there was more to come as we returned to the Matchetts' country cottage with its thick cobb walls and flagstone floors. Seated at the scrubbed pine table beside the tiny window, I was spoilt by Mrs Matchett with all kinds of country fayre – boiled eggs (from the Matchetts' own hens), home-baked bread and cakes, and, in season, enormous, juicy strawberries. While I feasted, Dad and Mr Matchett would sit around a blazing peat fire – always alight for it was cool within those thick walls – and with the smoke from Mr Matchett's pipe curling up towards the low, beamed ceiling, they would talk of the old days and good times and faded dreams. It was not melancholy talk; always there was laughter, and sometimes they would include me, such as the time they got round to talking country recipes – in particular, duck soup.

I'd never heard of duck soup before, so I enquired as to how it was made.

Mr Matchett, with just a hint of a twinkle in his eye, told me that in years gone by he and Dad had made this special dish on many occasions, right at this very fireplace. It wasn't easy, he said. 'First you had to get a pot boiling over the fire, then you had to add all the vegetables and keep stirring.'

'But what about the duck, Mr Matchett?'

He allowed himself a small smile. 'That was the tricky part, son. You had to choose a still night for this soup, and you had to make it at the right time of the evening – around dusk.'

Innocently, I asked why, and he explained that you had to wait for the ducks to come flying back to their nesting grounds on the shore of the lough.

'That's right,' Dad chipped in. 'And as soon as you heard them flying overhead you had to stick your shotgun up the chimney and let fly.'

'Sure enough,' grinned Mr Matchett, 'a plump duck would come straight down the chimney and land in the pot. And there it was – duck soup!'

Such are the memories that colour my own past, and I believe that my life now is the richer because of them. Not that such memories are remarkable in themselves, except perhaps for the fact that my father features so prominently in them. Would I have turned out the same, I wonder, if Dad had not been there gently to guide and fill those hours? Would Ben Forde be a very different person had he been left to find his own amusements and to develop his own (or someone else's) values? Would the seeds of faith planted in my young heart by my mother have been nurtured without the thoughtfulness and sharing of time which I received from my father?

There are other rewards, too. Because of the time we spent togther as man and boy, Dad and I are still close today. It seems we still have a lot to share together, and when circumstances allow I am not slow to seek out his company. From Dad's point of view, I suppose this is what is meant by the saying, 'If you hunt with your son when he is young, you won't have to look for him when he is older.'

I couldn't help thinking of these words as I drove back down to Castlereagh the morning after the fishing trip with Clive. Yet it wasn't my own son who was on my mind; it was young Donald, the lad I'd had to interview about his possible involvement in a murder; the lad who had refused to co-operate and given me nothing but abuse. No, that was not true; he had at least given me a clue as to why he had turned out this way.

Reporting to my Duty Inspector that morning I was informed that Donald was still in custody and that I was to take up the interview again. I can't say the prospect excited me, but away I went and made arrangements for the lad to be brought upstairs. A few minutes later we were facing each other across the table again, and looking through the notes of the officer who had been questioning him during my day off I did not feel very hopeful that the usual line of inquiry was going to get us anywhere.

Six hours of talking to myself proved me right. Donald's lips were buttoned up and it seemed that nothing would coax him to open them, not even when I digressed from the official line of inquiry to bring a little light relief with the tale of how my son took me fishing. No one could say I didn't try to reach that boy.

Six o'clock that evening saw me turning the last corner on the way home, and as always I was glad to be back in the place where I can relax awhile and forget about police business. This night, however, as Lily detected, I'd brought some of my work home with me.

'You're quiet,' she said as we set to washing the dishes after tea. 'What's on your mind, Ben?'

I smiled at her, thankful that she'd asked. 'It's a young lad I've been interviewing,' I said, and I told her just about all there was to tell about Donald.

'Ah well, you did your best,' she remarked. 'But it does make you wonder how youngsters turn out that way.'

'Oh, I think I know the answer to that,' I told her. 'You see, as far as I can make out, Donald's father was never much of a fisherman.'

Lily stared at me blankly. 'What does that have to do with it?'

'Quite a lot,' I said. 'At least, I think it does. Let me put the kettle on and I'll tell you all about it.'

6: Captured rebels

It was a frosted January evening and in the main CID office at my East Belfast police station the air hung thick with cigarette smoke as more than twenty detectives gathered for an unscheduled conference. It's not often that we're called together in such numbers, so we'd guessed that something was up. Our superior officers soon put us out of our misery.

It all revolved around a man named Kevin, a self-confessed former member of the IRA and one-time active terrorist who had recently walked into Musgrave Street Police Station and given himself up. Apparently he had become a Christian several years earlier and had now decided to make a clean breast of things, resulting in a full statement to the police. In that statement he had named other members of the IRA and their crimes, and that afternoon those men had been arrested. They were now in custody, awaiting questioning, and this was why we had been assembled. There were ten men; each was to be interviewed by two detectives. However, we were to be sure to understand that these men would be charged regardless of their degree of co-operation, on the strength of Kevin's evidence.

That Kevin had turned himself in was, of course, good news, but I was particularly pleased to learn that his change of direction had come as a result of his faith. This prompted me to approach the senior officer who had conducted the conference to see if there was anything I could do from the Christian angle. 'Perhaps I could talk with him, sir, and –'

'You'll do nothing of the sort, Forde.' The rebuff came from an even more senior officer who had overheard my suggestion. 'You've brought quite enough attention to yourself recently with that article in the Sunday paper,' he went on. 'Just keep out of it. You're likely to get yourself into trouble otherwise.'

I was disappointed at this reaction, but I knew that my CO meant well and headed for the cells.

He had hit upon a sore point. I had indeed suffered some adverse publicity in the press. Even though I had not been named in the article, its title – 'Interrogation by Bible' – and caustic comments could hardly have been aimed at anyone else. Somebody somewhere did not like what I was doing and had deliberately exaggerated my occasional Christian line of approach to an interviewee to make it sound as though I was in the habit of extracting confessions by lambasting suspects with threats of hell-fire and damnation if they didn't come clean.

I admit that the article hurt – though the sting lost its power once I'd put the attack into perspective – but, perhaps more importantly, my superior officer had a point: adverse publicity was one thing both I and the force could do without.

Accepting the decision, I put away my thoughts of extending any sort of Christian help to Kevin and got on with the job of interviewing one of the men arrested on the strength of his disclosures. Not surprisingly, the suspect said nothing to incriminate himself, but he was charged anyway, just as the CO had said.

Kevin, however, would not disappear from my thoughts, partly because of the curiosity that stirred within me. For years I had prayed that my God would infiltrate and change the life of even just one hard-line terrorist – just one black-hearted man – but, to be honest, as time had gone on and the troubles had become worse, I had begun to doubt whether such a thing would ever happen, particularly when I read in the Scriptures that 'if the good news is hidden from anyone it is hidden from the one who is on the road to eternal death'. Perhaps the truth was that such men would never change – that peace would never come to Northern Ireland by this means – and in fact I was only fooling myself to think otherwise.

But Kevin put paid to that line of thought – assuming he really was a changed man – and once my faith had begun to operate in this area again I acknowledged with fresh enthusiasm God's power to change lives, including those who had rebelled against God's laws to the extreme.

I recalled again those powerful words of St Paul's: 'I use God's mighty weapons not those made by men to knock down the devil's strongholds. With these weapons I can capture rebels and bring them back to God, and change them into men whose hearts' desire is obedience to Christ.'

Kevin was a rebel all right – he later received a life sentence for murder and other terrorist offences. Had God really captured him? If so, it was the least I could do to make myself known to him as a fellow Christian and to offer him any spiritual help that was in my power to give.

The problem was, the only way to Kevin was through my CO, and only a few days had passed since he'd told me to keep away from the man. Would he change his mind if asked to reconsider?

In such circumstances I am always conscious of my lowly position within the force (Detective Constable) and of the fact that I have little influence or ability in certain areas; yet at the same time I am aware of God's strength at work within me, and by walking in that strength I have seen God open many doors. The secret, I've learned, is in following the Bible's teaching: 'Trust the Lord completely; don't ever trust yourself.' When motivated by his Spirit, as I believed I was on the morning when I motored down to Castlereagh to seek permission to visit Kevin, I have found those words to be pure wisdom.

'All right,' said the officer after I'd explained my reasons for the visit. 'Providing you confine the conversation to Christian matters, I can see no harm in it.'

That suited me fine, of course, and after expressing my thanks I went off to make arrangements for the meeting. Two days later, along with a colleague, I was facing Kevin across a table in a small room at Crumlin Road Prison.

There is always a certain amount of restraint at such first meetings because whilst I might be there because I'm a Christian, I am still a member of the security forces and that has implications for both of us. From the prisoner's side, he might be glad to make my acquaintance as a Christian, but he may also have to contend with a deep-seated suspicion towards the representatives of law and order. Old enmities die hard, even when a man has decided to confess his crimes.

Such were the reservations we felt, both Kevin and I, as we began talking about Christian things. As so often before, *Hope in 'Bomb City'* proved to be a good starting point. Kevin had read the book and found it helpful. From my side, I was able to tell him that whilst in Berlin for a Christian rally I had met a friend of his from Dublin.

Gradually, of course, the level of conversation deepened, and it wasn't long before Kevin was telling me about his faith. As we'd already heard, he had committed his life to Christ about five years earlier. This followed his disillusionment with violence as the way forward for Northern Ireland, and came as the result of time spent with a group of Christians in Holland. He had seen how real Christ was in the lives of these people and was assured by them that the Saviour offered everything a sinner could want: forgiveness, peace, and a home in heaven. One night, of his own free will, he had gone to the cross, repented of his sins, taken Christ as his saviour, and got off his knees a new man.

Since then, he said, Christ had brought great changes to his life, and I commented that such was evident by the fact that he and I were now talking together within the walls of a prison.

He nodded, thoughtfully. The decision to turn himself in had not come easily, he explained, but he was convinced that this was the way that God would have him go, and as a result he had an inner peace.

I appreciated hearing this and was tempted to remark that it had taken courage to give himself up, knowing that he would likely spend many years in a cell, but then I realised that courage was the wrong word. This was an act of obedience. And it was at that moment that I received the assurance I had hoped for. It came to me quite clearly. Kevin *was* one of those captured rebels St Paul had talked about; one of those changed men whose hearts' desire is obedience to Christ.

Here was a mighty lesson and a tremendous encouragement. More importantly, perhaps it was also a significant breakthrough; a speck of light at the end of a long, dark tunnel. Kevin's conversion had nothing to do with me, of course, but that didn't matter. The fact was that he had been turned around by the power of the gospel – the same gospel I sought to live out in my life day by day – and now I knew that it was only a matter of time before it captured other rebels, too.

I left the prison that day assured that there was nothing else I could do for Kevin at that time, and glad to know that I was not alone in expressing concern for his spiritual welfare. The prison chaplain was visiting him regularly, and he also had contact with one or two Christian workers. This was good, for having informed on his fellow terrorists he had made plenty of enemies. Now he would need all the friends he could get.

This all happened some time ago and Kevin is now serving his prison sentence in Crumlin Road jail. I hear of him from time to time and occasionally write to him, perhaps enclosing some Christian literature that I think might be of help. I don't say a great deal about such developments at home, however, for while Lily is generally supportive, on this matter she and I have agreed to disagree. I well remember a conversation that took place one evening after we'd visited a widow and her children not many weeks after the husband and father had been murdered by terrorists. On the way home the subject of forgiveness came up and I mentioned the hope that I believe is extended to all men – murderers included – through the gospel. Lily was not slow to express her own view.

'It seems all wrong,' she said, 'that a man can commit murder and cause so much grief to a family, and then find peace and forgiveness while that family has to suffer in sorrow day after day. I find that hard to accept, Ben. It just doesn't seem fair.'

'I understand how you feel, Lily,' I replied, 'but who are we to discriminate? The gospel says that "*whoever* shall call on the name of the Lord shall be saved", and that has to be true. Besides, such men need changing, and if we're to see them put away their guns I believe that only Christ can do that.'

'But *murderers* . . .'

'Aye, I know it's hard to come to terms with that, especially when you've seen folks shed tears as we have tonight, but *I* could have turned out to be a murderer, given different circumstances. This evil thing that's hanging over us is powerful, Lily, and I have to be thankful that I've been kept from it. There but for the grace of God go I. But I'll tell you this – if I *had* turned out like that, and such a crime was playing on my mind, I'd be more than glad to learn that I could be forgiven.'

'I suppose so,' she said, but I knew that I hadn't convinced her. Maybe I had a different perspective on these things because I was having to deal with these men day after day and I saw them not simply as murderers but as fellow human beings who'd committed a crime. To my way of thinking that was a big difference.

Over the years I have had to think this issue through and I honestly believe that the only valid response to these people is the one which involves the grace of God. Perhaps it is best summed up in those words found in the letter of Jude: 'Hate every trace of their sin while being merciful to them as sinners.' If that is *God's* attitude, I really don't see how mine can be anything less.

However, I do not see myself as some sort of prisoners' good Samaritan, binding up the spiritual wounds of every offender I happen upon in my daily round. Though I'm willing to be of assistance, I do not normally go out of my way to make contact with such people, for I know my place and do not suffer any delusions about myself or my ability.

I cannot stop prisoners or suspects approaching *me*, however, and over the years, especially since publication of my first book, I have occasionally been asked if I would be willing to visit some of these people. The requests have come for a variety of reasons. None has been more surprising than that which prompted a message from a 'lifer' named Jimmy.

It began with a shout from Alfie, our office manager, as I entered the squad room late one afternoon, just as he was knocking off. 'Ben, there's a message in the book for you.'

I went over to the duty book and read: 'Contact Mr Rodgers, Assistant Governor, Crumlin Road Prison.' I glanced at the clock – it had gone five – but I thought I'd try the number anyway. Mr Rodgers was still there.

'It's about one of the prisoners,' he explained, and mentioned his name. 'He's doing life for murder.'

'How can I help, Mr Rodgers?'

'He's put in a request to speak with you. I understand that he's a Christian and believes that you can help him clear up some matter that's on his mind. There's no urgency, but when you get time I'd appreciate it if you could see him.'

I said I would do what I could and that I would put in a request for authorisation to see Jimmy. This I did the following day and permission was granted for a visit on 1st April. I remember this not simply because it was All Fools' Day (when I succeeded in playing April Fool on Keri and Clive) but also because that is the date of our wedding anniversary. On that occasion Lily and I were celebrating fifteen very happy years and a little celebration was planned around the evening meal, but first it was away into the city and a day's routine, including the promised visit to Crumlin Road.

On these occasions I usually take a colleague along and that day I asked my old pal Eddie if he would join me. Eddie and I have known each other for more than twenty years, since we served together as raw recruits down in the border town of Pettigo, and though he does not share my beliefs he knows me well enough now not to be embarrassed by anything I might say to a prisoner or anyone else as an expression of my faith.

Before meeting Jimmy, though, we needed to speak with Mr Rodgers who was going to detail the background to the prisoner's request.

'He's served eight years of a life sentence,' the Assistant Governor told us, 'and during that time he has committed his life to Christ.' As he spoke I was soon to realise that Mr Rodgers himself was a Christian, and that his own faith had helped him assess Jimmy's. 'As far as I can tell,' he went on, 'the man is sincere, and reports from the chaplains and prison staff appear to support this. Aside from his conversion, he has been a model prisoner and is seen to have dissociated himself from the paramilitaries.' Apparently Jimmy was formerly a member of the UVF (Ulster Volunteer Force), and it was for a murder committed whilst serving in that illegal organisation that he was now in prison.

I was glad to hear all this, of course – Jimmy sounded like another 'captured rebel', this time from the Loyalist side – but where did I fit in?

68

'As I said, he's read your book,' Mr Rodgers went on, 'and in you he sees a member of the RUC that he feels he can trust. It seems there are unconfessed crimes that he now wants to get cleared up with the police.'

'That sounds fair enough,' I said, 'and it would certainly tie in with his claim to be a Christian.'

Mr Rodgers nodded, yet there was concern in his eyes. 'There's something else, too. He is now saying that he is innocent of the murder of which he was convicted and he's asking for a retrial. He may be looking for your support in that area.'

'I see.'

'It's not necessarily as clear cut as that, of course,' he continued. 'Much as I see consistency in this man's life, one has to be careful. They have all the time in the world here to scheme and plan all types of moves. You and I both have been caught out before now. Still, go on and speak to him, and if you wouldn't mind I'd be glad if you would let me know how you get on.'

I appreciated Mr Rodgers' frank appraisal of the situation. True enough I'd been caught out by seemingly well-intentioned characters more than once, and it was only right to approach Jimmy with a certain amount of caution, if not scepticism. As we went down to the visiting area, following a prison officer through one set of security doors after another, it was with a prayer for wisdom.

Eventually the prison officer left us, and while we waited for the prisoner to arrive Eddie and I discussed how to approach him. With some amusement we recalled learning the textbook guidelines on such matters during our training at Enniskillen Police Depot. 'Courtesy is an essential quality and one that will smoothe many a pathway' was the first line, and idly we wondered whether today's recruits were still fed the same advice. The principle still held good, of course, but we were now living in a different world from that of the relatively peaceful 1960s. The troubles had spawned some evil, violent men and some of them wouldn't recognise courtesy even if it was labelled. Still, this certainly seemed the way forward with the man we'd come to see, and when eventually he arrived we put the old rule into operation.

The formalities over, we eased into a conversation about our apparently mutual faith – again through reference to my books – and among the many things Jimmy shared was his attendance at a thriving Bible class in D Wing. I appreciated hearing this, not only because I knew how important it was for any Christian to receive regular Bible teaching, but also because Lily and I had played a part in the commencement of that Bible class when, several years earlier, we had left a dozen copies of our daily study notes with the assistant chaplain in that wing.

All this, however, was by the way. Although I was curious to know just how sincere was Jimmy's faith, the main reason for the visit was to discuss his unconfessed crimes and his application for reinvestigation of the murder.

On the first point, which he said included the attempted murder of three Roman Catholics, I was ready and willing to help; on the second, I had my doubts and made no secret of them. I'd looked into the case a little and understood that Jimmy was in prison because he was found guilty of the murder of a man on a South Belfast housing estate in 1975. Wasn't that so?

That was correct, he told us, but he insisted that he did not commit that murder, and that he had only pleaded guilty on someone else's advice.

I had a job to swallow that one. Who in their right mind would plead guilty to a murder they did not commit? Even if that was true, why had he waited eight years to request a retrial?

He replied that the matter of serving time did not come into it, for he believed that he deserved to be in prison for the things he *had* done. He just wanted to clear the record of this particular crime.

That seemed a fair answer, though I was not completely satisfied. However, I would have to wait before discussing the matter further because our time was up. Wanting to finish on a positive note, I suggested we pray together, and hearing the way Jimmy addressed the Father went some way to justifying my willingness to believe that the man's faith was real. Time would tell.

Leaving the cells, Eddie and I reported back to Mr Rodgers, and after promising to do what I could we headed back to HQ. On the way we discussed these unusual circumstances and I was glad to have the benefit of Eddie's detached viewpoint. Not that he was negative, but he suggested I would do well to remember Mr Rodgers' words: 'They have all the time in the world here to scheme and plan all types of moves.'

He was right, of course. Perhaps Jimmy *didn't* kill that man and he genuinely wanted me to help him get the record straight, but was there also some other, sinister reason behind his sending for me? Was he just using me in some way?

As for his faith, I found myself asking questions about that, too. It seemed real enough, and yet in another sense such a dramatic change in a man seemed too good to be true. I found myself facing the same dilemma that had surfaced with Kevin's conversion. Yes, I'd been praying for this to happen for years, and had longed to see the power of the gospel revolutionise the lives of terrorists, but now that I was being offered proof that it was happening I had to ask myself whether or not I really believed it. Perhaps the answer lay in what Jesus himself said about those who professed to follow him: 'By their fruits shall you know them.' That was certainly the acid test for men who had committed murder (or attempted to) and now claimed to have been born again by the Spirit of God. As I said, time would tell, for fruit takes time to grow.

Meanwhile, I had agreed to give Jimmy assistance in being brought to trial for those unconfessed crimes, and after listening to him spelling out his offences during the visits I made to the Crumlin Road Prison over the ensuing months, I finally went through the official procedure of cautioning him and taking his statement in early October.

Another ten months were to pass before the court case, but at last the day arrived and Jimmy stood in the dock of Courtroom No. 4 charged with three counts of attempted murder, four armed robberies, possession of firearms, and theft of police uniforms. Enough charges to put a frown on any man in normal circumstances, but Jimmy appeared before the court with a smile of satisfaction on his flushed face. Clearly he was pleased at having these cases dealt with, and to have his conscience cleared.

I was glad for him, too, and optimistic of a just conclusion. Yet as I entered the witness box to give evidence of the prisoner's admissions I was aware that I would have to be honest in my replies, and it crossed my mind that the defence barrister might ask questions as to what I thought of the accused's conviction for murder. Though by now I was inclined to believe that he was innocent, I had nothing other than my intuition to go by, and intuition is not worth a great deal in a court of law.

I felt on firmer ground with the questions I suspected would come my way in connection with Jimmy's faith – and my own. Prior to the hearing the Queen's Counsel had requested a copy of *Hope in 'Bomb City'*, having learned that it was through this book that the accused had been prompted to contact me.

Several questions were asked as to my own faith and the sincerity of Jimmy's conversion whilst in prison, and I was glad to be able to respond positively on both counts.

(The involvement of the book in the trial, by the way, caused quite a bit of interest amongst some of the policemen in court that day, and when approached by one or two of them during the recession I was thankful of the opportunity to accommodate them with copies that

I'd brought with me that day in my brief-case. Such are the openings that God gives to spread the message of Christ in the places to which my job takes me.)

Echoing my own testimony of Jimmy's Christianity was the prison chaplain who explained that he had known the accused over a period of four years and in that time had found him to be consistent in his faith. The prisoner in the dock, he told the Judge, was now a different man from the one who had last appeared there charged with murder.

The court then adjourned while the Judge considered the case and prepared judgment. When we resumed, Jimmy was sentenced to nine years and six months, the sentence to commence from that date. He was delighted with the decision – a fact that was written all over his face – and his appreciation was expressed to me by his father who called out to me just as I was about to leave the court. 'Thanks, Mr Forde,' he said. 'Justice was done and seen to be done.'

It is a strange thing indeed to be thanked for helping to get someone a long prison sentence, but perhaps that says something about Northern Ireland. It could only happen here!

Five days after this case was wound up I received a telephone call at home from my former Detective Chief Inspector, Frank Dempsey, under whom I served in my Crime Squad days. It was partly a personal call, but after a while he came to the real business on his mind.

'Ben, there's a man on remand in Crumlin Road Prison on a murder charge and he says he wants to speak to you. Says he became a Christian three weeks ago. Will you see him?'

Behind me, sitting in the lounge and supposedly watching TV, was Lily. Over the years she has developed an amazing sort of radar that enables her to pick up the vibrations from any telephone call I receive, and within a few sentences of the conversation she is able to sense what's going on. Glancing at her on this occasion, my own radar sensed disapproval.

Promising to do what I could, I hung up and immediately was asked, 'What was that all about?'

Briefly, I explained.

'Ben, they're just using you. A man says he's been saved three weeks and now he expects everyone to jump. It's just too easy for someone to say he's changed when he's facing a murder charge. Talk of conversion is too cheap.'

I recalled a headline I'd read in the paper a while back: *'Conversions don't impress me,' says Judge*. He had been saying much the same thing as Lily, and I could see their point, especially when it may appear that a man is pleading conversion in order to secure a more lenient sentence.

But thinking back to Kevin whose conversion prompted him to give himself up to face a life sentence, and Jimmy, whose faith was behind his decision to clear his past of serious terrorist crimes, I can't lightly dismiss every new story of converted criminals as a defensive strategy. These men – these captured rebels – *are* being changed and they are not changing themselves. And for anyone who has the faith to believe it – including myself – there is at last the evidence that God is answering prayer and breaking down the devil's strongholds to bring the light of faith into what are perhaps some of the darkest corners of the world.

'Ah, Ben, you're just dreaming,' I can hear the sceptics cry. 'Tomorrow you'll wake up and see that it was nothing to get excited about.'

And I answer those cries the only way I know how. If I'm dreaming, let me dream on.

7: Chasing the rainbow

It's a sad comment on a policeman's life in Ulster that so much of his time is taken up with giving evidence in court. Such is the volume of crime – especially terrorist type crime – that visits to the courthouse have increasingly become the rule rather than the exception. This is not surprising when I reflect on the fact that since the present troubles began in 1969 more than 2,000 people have died by the bullet or the bomb. In that sense I have to be thankful for court appearances, for they mean that the perpetrators of these crimes are being brought to justice. On this particular Monday morning, however, I was not enthusiastic about driving down to the Crumlin Road for the beginning of yet another murder trial, for today was the funeral of a good friend and I was hoping to be able to attend.

Ex-Head Constable Walter Allen was a fellow Christian and had long been an inspiration to me in my faith. Readers of *Hope in 'Bomb City'* may recall that it was whilst I was a young uniformed police officer stationed at Comber that I first met Walter. He was my divisional CO, but I soon learned to think of him more as an older brother in Christ who was always quick to speak for his Saviour and to identify himself with those of the same faith, even if they were of lowly rank. But more than this, Walter was a great encourager and it was through his friendship and interest that I took my first step in witnessing publicly to my faith in the Lord Jesus Christ.

That was at a Youth for Christ rally in Killyleagh. Walter was to be the speaker and he asked me if I would accompany him, and perhaps say a few words about my faith as a young policeman. I remember it as a rather nerve-racking experience – I'd never spoken in public before – but now I look back on the occasion with thankfulness, for I know that all the opportunities I have had over the years to witness from the platform would not have been possible without that first faltering step. For that reason I would always be thankful to Walter, and when I heard that my good friend had died (of natural causes) I was keen to get to the funeral.

'Maybe they'll call you to give evidence early,' Lily suggested over breakfast that morning. 'Then you'll be able to get away in good time.'

I hoped so, and later as I stopped at the court's car park barrier for the usual search before being admitted I calculated that if I could be finished there by 12.30 I would still be in time to drive the eleven miles to Newtownards for the service.

But that was soon looking unlikely. Up the steps I went, past the towering stone pillars and in through the main doors, only to be told by a court official that the judge had been delayed and wouldn't arrive until 11.30.

With time now on my hands I decided to return to the car and review the evidence I would give. Experience has taught me that it pays to look ahead and try to anticipate the sort of questions the Defence Counsel may ask, and also to take note of any pitfalls that should be avoided in my answers. So much hung on the evidence presented to the court, and though it was but a few short steps from the Crumlin Road Courthouse to the Crumlin Road Prison (directly opposite each other and linked by an underground tunnel) it was never a foregone conclusion that the man in the dock would later be taking those steps to the beginning of a prison sentence, no matter how conclusive the evidence of his crimes appeared. An astute barrister could change all that.

76

But at least he could not influence the jury, for in cases of this kind there never was a jury to influence. There used to be, of course, but in recent years it had become increasingly dangerous for members of the public to be involved in terrorist trials, and following threats on people's lives and other forms of interference by terrorist agencies, the courts had now resorted to the Diplock system (named after Judge Diplock) in which the presiding judge had to weigh up the evidence before him and pronounce the verdict solely on his own initiative.

This was another sad comment on life in Northern Ireland, and though it was not the most satisfactory means of judgment, and sharply increased the dangers to the judge's own life, it was perhaps necessary if these offenders were to be punished.

The system did, of course, speed up the proceedings somewhat, and for this reason I remained faintly hopeful of getting away in time for the funeral. But when the court was adjourned for lunch at one o'clock, and I still hadn't been called to the witness stand, I gave up any thoughts of making it to Newtownards to pay my last respects to Walter Allen.

Yet, as it turned out, instead of my going to Walter that lunchtime, there was a sense in which Walter came to me.

Heading out of the courtroom I made for the snack bar in the main hallway to secure a couple of sausage rolls and a black tea, and it was there in the queue that I was joined by Dougie, a sergeant whom I'd known since we were stationed together at Lisburn Road many years ago.

'How's things, Ben?'

'Not so bad, Dougie,' I said, and went on to explain my disappointment about Walter's funeral. From there we moved to the usual things – the job, our children, their future – and it was somewhere in there, amidst the everyday things of life, that memories of Walter surfaced again. For Walter was essentially a practical Christian and he believed that faith in Christ was a dynamic that touched – or should touch – every area of our lives.

After a while Dougie asked, 'But what *is* faith?'

In response, Walter's own definition came to mind, for he had a most lucid and memorable way of explaining the driving force of his life. There in the courthouse hallway, amidst the barristers and the sausage rolls, I told Dougie about it.

'I can see him now,' I said, 'standing in a gospel meeting and answering that very question. He used to raise his left hand, with his fingers splayed out, and one by one he would grasp each finger with his other hand as he spelt out the word "faith", one finger for each letter – F-A-I-T-H. To him it meant, Forsaking All, I Take Him.'

Later that day, my evidence now behind me, that memory of Walter was to be stirred again as I reflected on this whole issue of faith in 'Bomb City'. Walter was right, of course, about the receiving side of faith; without that there would be no faith at all. But there was another side to it – a side which Walter fully understood and which was reflected in his whole Christian manner – the side of giving. Not simply the giving of money to God's work, though that was important, but the giving of ourselves to whatever sphere of service the Lord laid before us. Faith, after all, was hardly faith if it didn't result in action. As the Bible says, 'Faith without works is dead.' From my own experience I knew that this whole area of Christian 'works' sometimes posed difficulties because of the sheer enormity of the problems which needed tackling. In the face of such enormous needs one man's contribution seemed meaningless and fostered the false notion that probably it was better not to get involved than to spend a lifetime scratching at the surface of a problem I couldn't change anyway.

The issue was highlighted one day in my *Every Day with Jesus* Bible reading notes. There, author Selwyn Hughes succinctly stated the problem: 'Many Christians refuse to do anything because they can't do everything. Because they can't set the world on fire, they refuse to light a candle. Because they can't save the world, they refuse to save a single soul.' But what was the answer? Selwyn went on, 'Love is doing the little thing at hand, thus opening the way for the bigger thing in the future.'

These words were a great encouragement to me in my own efforts as a Christian, particularly in my endeavours to light a candle in the dark world of terrorism. For me, this was 'the thing at hand', yet the scale of the problem was so vast that it was daunting. Could one man bring radical change to a situation which was the product of a long and bitter history? I knew the answer to that – no! – but maybe, just maybe, I could spark a flame.

The idea – which had grown into a conviction over the years – was that there was another way of fighting crime in Northern Ireland, particularly terrorist-type crime. For a very long time the police force had been battling against the terrorists through the established means of detection and prevention of crime, and for twenty-odd years I had been part of that machine. Knowing that we had made little headway in stemming this evil tide, and at times being accused of widening the sectarian divide rather than closing it, I had come to the conclusion that there was room for an alternative method – that of building bridges. I called it 'Criminal Caring'.

Basically, the idea was to form a front-line link between the RUC and the terrorist/criminal fraternity, based on the building of relationships which would lead to a better understanding between both groups. The object, as I saw it, was to develop those relationships on a personal basis with the ultimate hope of reconciling the two parties. If this could be achieved it seemed there was every possibility of encouraging former criminals to become useful members of society, working *with* the community instead of against it.

This was not some 'pie in the sky' idea that I'd dreamed up in an idle moment; over the years I had been putting the idea into operation on a small personal scale, and I'd seen enough encouragements to make me believe that, given the right people from both sides, a large degree of success was possible.

Of course, I was aware that to some of my colleagues such a proposal would seem to have no place in community policing, and some would even think it a ridiculous suggestion. On the other hand I knew that I wasn't alone in seeing positive results when a degree of caring was shown to those involved in crime. Those of my colleagues who had taken the trouble to interest themselves in the problems of some of their criminal contacts would, I knew, bear me out that such an investment of time and consideration often paid dividends.

Before submitting such a proposal to my superiors, however, I felt I should raise the subject with someone who was outside of the force yet who understood policing and would be able to give me an honest appraisal of the idea. When the name of retired Assistant Chief Constable William Meharg came to mind, I knew he was just the man. When I'd formulated my thoughts more clearly, and had typed up a basic outline, I rang Mr Meharg and asked if he would see me. He agreed. But driving to his home one Friday evening in January, 1981, and about to share the vision of Criminal Caring for the first time, I did wonder what this experienced police officer's reaction would be. Maybe I was just chasing the rainbow.

Yet I had to press forward – had to at least try to light that candle – and as we settled in Mr Meharg's lounge before a blazing coal fire, I began to outline what I visualised as a new branch of the RUC, probably operating within the jurisdiction of the Criminal Investigation Department.

'You see, sir,' I began, 'I believe there is a place for extending a hand of friendship to certain offenders, certain suspects, certain people whose time in prison is up, in the belief that they may well respond favourably.'

'Those who show willing when approached, you mean.'

'That's right. I'm convinced there are many people, particularly on the fringes of crime, terrorist and otherwise, who would welcome the opportunity to re-establish themselves in society, and I believe they could do it if they had the support of a group such as Criminal Caring. I'm sure such support would be welcomed by their families, too.'

He nodded, but said, 'You'd meet with a lot of suspicion, of course. Some people would think this was merely a softly, softly approach – another means to secure convictions.'

I told him I realised that; that initially there was bound to be a great deal of wariness in certain quarters. 'But in time we could prove that this was a genuine attempt by the community's police force to make a valid contribution in an area of concern not normally associated with the RUC. And maybe we'd get some good publicity for a change. I do think the image is important, not just for us as members of the force, but for the man in the street whose interests we are meant to be serving.'

Mr Meharg sat silently for a moment, glancing down the report I'd given him. 'What about the man who had become deeply involved in terrorism but now wanted out? How would you go about helping him?'

I'd already thought about this. 'It would be difficult, I know, because such a man would not want to be seen associating with the police in any way. But maybe assistance could be given through a third party, at least until the man was able to break away from the paramilitaries, if that was his wish. If they were serving a prison sentence at the time of contact, though, I suppose direct dialogue would be possible. The main thing would be to establish the link, and that could come from either party, so long as the people who wanted help knew that it was available.'

My retired superior eyed me for a moment, then said, 'Who would contribute to such a branch, should it be formed?'

'Essentially police officers,' I replied, 'probably chosen from within the CID because we are the people who come face to face with the criminal element day by day. Probably no one outside of their own circle knows them better than we do, and there is already something of a relationship there, whether that relationship is acknowledged or not. The important thing would be for members of the department to have a genuine concern for the well-being of their contacts, regardless of their religious or political background, or the nature of their crimes.'

'And the type of help you foresee being offered?'

'All types, sir. Practical, mental, spiritual – whatever was called for, or requested.'

Mr Meharg leaned back in his chair, nodding thoughtfully. Then he settled to reading more of my outline, and after that we talked some more, covering just about every angle of this proposal. I hadn't expected such a long session, I'll admit, but I was thankful that this former high-ranking officer was taking my suggestions seriously and exploring them thoroughly. It had gone ten o'clock when our discussion drew to a close before that warming fire.

'Well, I'll admit you've set me thinking, Ben,' Mr Meharg told me. 'I believe you have something worth pursuing in this idea of Criminal Caring, and I'd like to discuss it with some senior officers still serving with the force. But I think you already know that launching such an idea would be fraught with difficulties, and then there's the other hurdle of the proposal's gaining acceptance out there on the streets. That presents problems, too.'

I said that I understood, and that I would be most surprised if there *weren't* problems; in our line of work we'd come to expect them. 'Besides my own experience is that it's *through* our problems – personal and national – that we can grow together. That's our common ground, after all, and I think the situation offers many possibilities for mutual help, if we're willing to get involved. And why shouldn't we? If you'll permit me to say so, sir, I don't think anyone can pretend that the RUC is without blame – we're human and bound to make mistakes, just like everyone else – and personally I believe that we need to recognise that we are part of the problem before we can effectively become part of the answer. To my mind that's the spirit which could bring Criminal Caring into being. I really believe that such an arm of the law – a new, caring arm – could make a positive contribution to peace in this land of ours.'

Mr Meharg smiled. 'Well, we'll have to wait and see. Let me talk to my colleagues, and then perhaps we can meet again.'

Almost four years have passed since that first meeting with Ex-Assistant Chief Constable Meharg, but apart from submitting an official proposal to my superiors and having the occasional discussion on the subject, little has happened to further the idea of Criminal Caring as a working reality in our troubled community.

Will it ever come to pass? Humanly speaking, it seems unlikely, but I believe that the initial idea was God-inspired and so I am content to leave the outcome to him. I do not pretend to understand his plan or his purposes, only that he is to be trusted. Over the years I have learned that whether or not I can see the end from the beginning doesn't really matter, providing I am obedient to that inner voice and seeking to walk in the path he sets before me.

In this respect I'll be in good company, for my Bible tells me that when Abraham was told by God to leave his home and go far away to another land which God would give him, *he trusted God*. Away he went, not even knowing where he was going. I know how it feels!

But that is the adventurous nature of faith, and in it there is a divine security which only those who abandon themselves to God will know. Where that adventure will take me is, of course, unknown, but judging from past experience I can safely say that the road will always be a narrow one. Unpopular, too. For like the poet I came to a crossroads in a wood and took the road less travelled by. This means that I am sometimes misunderstood, and perhaps from time to time thought to be chasing rainbows. But what matter? For this road, with all its sudden twists and upward turns, will someday lead me home.

8: Bombshell

As a member of the security forces in Northern Ireland it is essential that I tread carefully in the places where my job takes me, seeking always to be on the alert lest I unwittingly step into some lurking danger. This attitude is one which our instructors seek to instill in us during training, and which is later developed through practical experience in real-life situations as we go about our work. For my own part this sense of caution was shaped and honed in the border areas where, during my first few years of police service, I frequently had the palm-sweating task, along with my colleagues, of searching culverts and other likely places for hidden explosives.

This was an aspect of mental preparedness that I took very seriously – and still do – for it's a nerve-jangling fact that you need to step on a land-mine only once to trigger it. If you're careless – or just plain unfortunate – you'll get the full force of the bomb in your face.

But not all bombshells are made of literal explosives. Some are simply written on paper.

It was the morning after my session with Mr Meharg and I was down at Castlereagh interviewing a suspect about the murder of a soldier in Londonderry. It was a tragic case; a young guardsman on leave had returned to that area on personal business (he'd married a local girl) and he made the mistake of entering the wrong public house for a drink. There the Provisional IRA shot him dead.

My assignment that day was to question a likely suspect, but after a fruitless few hours I decided to break off and head home for a quick lunch. Over hot soup and rolls Lily produced a letter which had arrived that morning, and as I opened it and began to read I felt as though someone had just lit a fuse inside my head.

'What is it?' Lily asked, sensing my annoyance.

I handed her the letter. 'It's from solicitors. Their client seems to think I still owe them something.' (The details are unimportant. Suffice to say that if these people didn't get what they wanted they would sue me. I was aware that they thought they had a justified complaint against me and I'd been in touch with them. In fact I'd complied with their request to put matters right and they had seemed satisfied. But now they were saying something quite different, and in my view their present action was totally unwarranted.)

Lily scanned the letter, then stared at me. 'But I thought this was all cleared up,' she said. 'Didn't you speak to these people on the phone?'

'I did, and I thought that was the last we'd hear. But now . . .' I looked at her across the table. The soup was getting cold. 'I don't know what the Lord's trying to teach us this time,' I said, 'but it looks like it could be an expensive lesson.'

Driving back to Castlereagh that afternoon I was not in a good frame of mind, and throughout the further interview with the IRA suspect and the eventual return home I felt oppressed. My life amidst the terrorists brought quite enough stresses and strains without having to endure pressures from other areas. And I had plenty of court cases to think about without having one of my own. Not surprisingly, my initial prayer on the matter was a familiar one. *You got me into this, Lord, and you'll have to get me out of it.*

Yet, as I reflected on the situation later that evening, I was aware that whenever my God had allowed adverse circumstances in the past it had always been for some specific purpose, and despite the bad taste left in my mouth by that letter I was conscious that the Lord was in control and that he wouldn't allow anything to touch his children which he couldn't use for their blessing and his glory.

There was comfort to be had from that, just as there was comfort in the scriptures that came to my attention before I turned in that night. In Ephesians I read, 'Christ himself is our way of peace,' and in Philippians, 'It is he (God) who will supply all your needs from his riches in glory, because of what Christ Jesus has done for us.'

Such verses are empty without faith, of course, but as I let these words sink in I knew that I *believed* them; knew that, through them, God was speaking to *me*.

Naturally, I would endeavour to put matters right with these people, but if for any reason things should not work out and I ended up paying out money, I could rest assured that the Lord would provide for our needs.

This conviction was so strong that, just two days later, I made a financial commitment that would not have been possible if faith had not been operating in my life.

It was the Sunday afternoon and I was alone in the house. Lily had driven Keri and Clive to their Bible class and I was enjoying a rare hour of relaxation with my feet up. On the cassette player a testimony tape was playing, and as I lounged on the settee I listened to what the speaker, George Bates, had to say. Among the many things he shared was reference to a friend of his, a man by the name of David Ravey. And at this point my mind began to wander, for I knew of David Ravey, now deceased, through his daughter, Mrs Claire Erwin. Only a few months earlier Claire and her husband Andy had visited our home and, along with Lily, we had sat talking in this very room.

The Erwins, we'd learned, were responsible for running the Wayside Home for handicapped people in Donaghadee – a work started by David Ravey some years before – and now Claire was in the process of writing up her father's story. Their visit was in order to seek help in getting such a story published. At the time I had encouraged Claire as much as I could, and I'd gladly shared with her what I had learned from my own experience of publishing, but I don't know that I was of any great help to her. Now, as I lay back with that conversation re-playing in my mind, I began to wonder whether I should offer to assist in Claire's project in a more tangible way.

One thousand pounds. The thought came to me quite abruptly and at first I was inclined to dismiss it. But it would not go away. A thousand pounds would go a long way towards helping Claire get her story published, and I had the means to help her. This was unusual, I should point out, but it was true that at that time I had a thousand pounds of the Lord's money sitting in the bank. Normally such moneys – the proceeds from the books and records – passed in and out quite quickly, as various needs were brought to my attention. But for some reason – for this very project? – the money had accumulated over the months and I was now in a position to pay out such a large amount, if that was what the Lord wanted.

I leaned over and switched off the cassette player. This needed some thinking about. With a possible court case hanging over our heads we would perhaps be unwise to release such a sum of money when we might need it for legal expenses, or whatever. Then again, we regarded ourselves as stewards of all that came our way – everything, including our very lives, were committed to our heavenly Father – and if it was his desire that we should part with that money we would not want to refuse. As for our security, our God was rich beyond measure, and providing we sought to walk in fellowship with him, we knew we would never miss out.

But a thousand pounds, Lord?

Philippians came smiling out of the shadows: 'He will supply all your needs . . .'

With a strangely glowing confidence I went to the telephone. 'Claire? Ben Forde.' I explained why I was ringing and, with a small swallow, mentioned the thousand pounds. 'I believe the Lord would have me do this to help you get your book out.'

'Why, Ben, that – that's just incredible. Hold on, will you, while I get Andy on the other phone. This is just wonderful.'

A moment or two later she explained why she was so excited. It wasn't just the money, but the fact that she saw the Lord's hand in it. Just that morning, she told me, she had been praying again about getting her story published, but felt very conscious of the many obstacles. She had prayed, too, about whether or not God would have her contact me again to discuss the matter further, and she had asked that he would confirm this one way or the other through that morning's service at her church. 'The answer came through George Bates' text,' she went on. 'It was from Job chapter twenty-two: "Acquaint now thyself with him and be at peace." Well, Ben, as that word was expounded I just knew that the Lord was saying I should go ahead and meet up with you again, and at the same time telling me that I should be at peace that he would open the way for the book to be published. I still felt hesitant about phoning you, though – but now I've no need, for here you are. This is wonderful!'

It was. And it was quite a relief, too, to know that in phoning Claire with the offer of financial help with the book I was following the Spirit's leading. When finally I put down the phone, having arranged to meet Claire and Andy at a later date in order to hand over the cheque, I had a great peace. What's more, the heaviness of the legal case had completely lifted. Quite irrational, of course, but I had long since learned that God's ways were not my ways, nor his thoughts my thoughts. Once again, I couldn't understand them, but I knew I was getting blessed by trusting him and letting him work out his purposes in his own way.

But although it's true that we walk by faith and not by sight, I've often found that in such circumstances the Lord is quick to encourage me with very visible evidences of his love and leading. On this occasion it was to be no different, as I discovered just two days after committing myself to parting with that large sum of money.

On the Monday, when I'd returned to Castlereagh to continue the interview with the suspected IRA man from Londonderry, I found a note on my desk asking me to contact a certain police widow whom I'll call Judy (she wishes to remain anonymous). There was no indication as to what this was about, and even after speaking to her on the phone that afternoon I was no wiser as to what was on her mind. She simply said that she would like to talk to me, and was there any chance that Lily and I could get up to see her within the next few days? As it happened, we were able to drive across town to her home the following afternoon, and after chatting generally for a while Judy came to the point.

'Ben, I wanted to see you because the Lord has laid something on my heart and it's to do with your book, *Hope in 'Bomb City'*. I think you already know that reading that book was a big help to me when I was getting over George's death. Did I tell you that?'

'You did,' I said. I well remembered the tragic circumstances; how gunmen had murdered Judy's husband when he was on duty one morning, leaving yet another Ulster family shattered with grief. It had been a great encouragement to me to know that, during that time, Judy had been helped by some of the things I'd shared in that first book.

'Well,' Judy went on, 'I've often wished that there was some way I could help get copies of that book out to other people who would benefit from its message, but I didn't know how. But just this week I received a cheque in the post – compensation in respect of George's death – and I believe the Lord would have

90

me use a portion of it to purchase copies of the book for prisons, schools, hospitals and the like, so that people who wouldn't normally buy the book – or perhaps can't afford it – can have a copy free of charge. So – here . . .' She leaned across and handed me a cheque, and I glanced at it. It was made out for two thousand pounds.

'Why, Judy,' I said, 'I don't know what to say.'

'You don't have to say anything, Ben,' she smiled. 'I believe that's God's book, even more than it's yours, and I just want to see it used.'

We had a cup of tea with Judy before we left, and on the way out I thanked her again. 'This will buy an awful lot of books,' I said. 'And I'll see to it that they're used wisely.'

Judy grinned. 'I think the Lord will see to that.' And of course she was right.

Driving home, Lily and I were rejoicing and thanking God. Judy's gift would have been an encouragement at any time, but right now, with our finances under attack, such a gesture was particularly significant. To us it seemed that through that solicitors' letter the enemy of our souls was seeking to steal our peace. For certain reasons Lily and I had come to the conclusion that the attack was connected with *Hope in 'Bomb City'*. Over the years we had seen our God bring many people out of darkness into his wonderful light as a direct result of that publication, and it was clear that Satan wasn't going to stand by and let that happen without striking back. But no sooner had he unleashed the blow than the Lord had rallied his support around us in the shape of Judy's loving gift. To us it was as though the Lord was saying, 'I'm right behind you. Don't let this attack undermine your peace; the victory is mine, and mine it will remain.'

Over the ensuing months this sense of the Lord's support remained with us and it was with a real aware- ness of his purpose that we purchased those books on

Judy's behalf – 2,250 copies at a special discount rate from the publisher. We then arranged for a special label to be affixed to the back of each book, explaining to the reader how their copy had come to be in their hands, free of charge.

During this time we had also sought to put matters right with the people who had threatened to take us to court, and we were hopeful that the issue would be cleared up fairly quickly. Unfortunately, however, there was a breakdown in communications and before many more weeks had passed we heard that I was to be served a legal writ. The case, it seemed, was to go ahead.

Remarkably, I still possessed that deep peace, even when I was handed the writ that demanded I prepare to do battle in the courts, but I confess that when I went for an initial meeting with Richard, my solicitor (recommended by a friend from church), that peace became a bit wobbly.

We met at Richard's house where he and his wife told me that they both had read the book and were glad to be able to help me at this time. I appreciated this, but I wasn't so thankful for Richard's assessment of what appeared to lie in store for me.

'You realise that this is a High Court writ and not a County Court one, do you, Ben?'

I nodded. 'It means they're using the big guns, doesn't it? That sounds expensive.'

'It is,' he said. 'Legal representation for a four-day hearing in the High Court could cost you around two and a half thousand pounds, not to mention the figure the plaintiff's solicitor will be looking for.'

I grimaced. 'How much is that likely to be?'

'Well, the fact that they're going to the High Court means they're automatically looking for at least five thousand pounds.'

At that point I was glad to be sitting down, and I was also thankful that Richard didn't elaborate. He didn't tell me then, but at a later stage I learned that a similar case had ended with the plaintiff being awarded £50,000.

At such times one has to be practical. 'I don't have that sort of money, Richard, and I don't know where I could get it, short of selling the house.'

He nodded thoughtfully. 'I'm sorry to say that's not out of the question, Ben. Alternatively, in the event of you losing such a case, and assuming you were unable to pay, the court would appoint an official to visit your home and assess your financial position with a view to making a recommendation to the court. It could mean a second mortgage, or possibly some other form of regular payment.'

I swallowed hard. If this was my own solicitor's assessment, I thought, I'd hate to hear the plaintiff's.

A few days later I met Richard again, this time more formally in his Bangor office overlooking the Irish Sea. Out there, above the choppy waves, dark storm clouds were gathering – a reflection, it seemed, of what was happening right there in that office. The outlook for Bangor and Ben Forde was about the same: bleak.

'I'm afraid it doesn't look too good for you,' Richard told me. 'The plaintiff appears to have a good case and if it goes to court they might very well win. If that happened, you'd be responsible for their legal costs, too.'

I looked at him across the desk. 'You said *if* the case goes to court. Is there a chance it won't?'

'Well, there's always the possibility of a settlement out of court, and we shall have to look into that. But in the meantime we're obliged to pursue the case through the legal system.'

There was not much of a spring in my step when I left Richard's office that morning, and as I headed off to my next appointment – a meeting with Andy and Claire Erwin – I told myself, not for the first time, that this was a crazy world. It certainly seemed crazy that just a few minutes from now I would be handing over to Claire that

93

promised cheque for a thousand pounds. Not that such a sum would go far towards meeting our costs if Richard's picture of gloom and doom should come to pass.

But it's remarkable what a difference good Christian fellowship can make even on the darkest of days, and as I sat with Andy and Claire in a coffee shop not far from Richard's office, sharing with them something of the legal matter confronting me, I began to feel the heaviness lifting. Claire, I'm glad to say, was in buoyant mood and her own testimony of God's provision for the Wayside Home was a tonic.

'Ben, I can't tell you how many miracles we've seen our God perform for us when we've needed money,' she beamed. 'Wayside has always been a faith work – we receive no grants or subscribed support – and we've yet to see the day when our God doesn't meet our every need.' She paused. 'So what if the very worst happens and you have to pay fifty thousand pounds – even a hundred thousand? Listen, our God will not see his children begging bread. Believe it, Ben – he *will* provide. Every penny.'

Those Bangor clouds had grown darker still as I drove up out of the town an hour or so later, but on the inside the outlook was definitely brighter.

At home I shared with Lily the gist of what Richard had told me that morning, softening the blow as much as I could. Then I told her about the meeting with Andy and Claire. 'When I left them, Claire suggested I read Psalms 20 and 21. Come and sit down and we'll look at them together.'

In the lounge we settled on the settee and I opened up my Bible. Psalm 20 began:

'In your day of trouble, may the Lord be with you!
May the God of Jacob keep you from all harm. May he
send you aid from his sanctuary in Zion. May he
remember with pleasure the gifts you have given him,
your sacrifices and burnt offerings. May he grant you

your heart's desire and fulfil all your plans. May there be shouts of joy when we hear the news of your victory, flags flying with praise to God for all that he has done for you. May he answer all your prayers!

I paused there and turned to Lily with a smile that seemed to come up from somewhere deep inside. Then I said: 'I don't think we're finished yet, love.'

9: Away from it all

Over the following months there was much to-ing and fro-ing of solicitors' letters, many telephone calls, and the occasional session with lawyers and barristers. The legal writ business was dragging on and the cost was mounting. From my own experience I knew that legal matters tended to be long-drawn-out affairs, and although that didn't particularly worry me (I had quite enough to occupy my mind with the daily round of police investigations), I felt frustrated by the financial uncertainty that we were forced to live with.

Claire had been quite right, we believed, when she had assured us that our God would supply our every need, but I felt that at the same time I had a responsibility to watch our personal spending. That seemed only sensible, and the issue was highlighted by the question of the family's summer holiday. Over recent years we'd been fortunate enough to be able to afford a trip abroad, and there was no doubt in my mind as to the value of such an away-from-it-all holiday, luxuriating in hotel accommodation and relaxing in the guaranteed sunshine. In my reckoning the cost was more than justified by the benefits of being so far removed from the pressures and physical dangers of the policeman's lot in Belfast. Such a measure of peace was, in my opinion, almost without price. But this year, it seemed, the cost would be too high.

'We'll have to forget Ibiza,' I told Lily as we took our lunch out into the garden one warm spring day. 'Much as

I'd like us to go, I think it would be better to save the money.'

'The kids won't much like the idea,' she said. 'You know how they love that warm sea. Still, it's for the best.'

I nodded. 'We'll get away somewhere, though. I don't see any sense in cutting out the holiday altogether. We need the break.' I paused, leaning back in my garden chair with my eyes closed and face up to the warming sun. 'I'm sure the Lord's got something for us, anyway.'

It was not simply a casual remark but another expression of faith. The Lord, we knew, was just as interested in our holidays as he was in the hurly-burly of our daily lives, and over the years we had learned to look to him for direction in this matter, too. And why not? He was far wiser than we were, and we knew that any holiday he planned for us was planned with all the care and consideration of a loving Father. I thought of that verse in the Psalms: 'You chart the path ahead of me, and tell me where to stop and rest.' Nothing was left to chance with the Lord. And even as we sat there munching our lunchtime snack, his plan for our summer break began to unfold. It came via the postman on his midday round.

'A letter from the MacLeods!' I sang as I fetched the mail from the doormat.

'Oh, good!' Lily returned, for we were always pleased to hear from our friends Murdo and Mary on the Isle of Lewis. The previous summer we'd spent a marvellous week with these dear people – our first visit to the Outer Hebrides – and any reminder of that grand holiday was welcome.

But Murdo's letter brought more than memories. 'They want us to go and stay with them again,' I said, reading through. 'For two weeks this time. And they say we're to be sure to come.' I turned to Lily. 'How about that?'

'Wonderful!' Her smile echoed the sentiment, and we both knew that Keri and Clive wouldn't need asking twice. I handed the letter to Lily.

'I think that's God's place for us this summer,' I said.

It was early July when we boarded the ferry at Larne – a bright summer's day packed with promise, just as our vessel was bulging with cross-channel travellers. Up on deck we looked out to sea, savouring the relaxing days that stretched out before us, and occasionally glancing back at the troubled homeland we were leaving. It is a beautiful land, there's no denying that, but it bears some tragic scars and we were glad to be leaving it behind for a while. Peace was what we needed, and sadly for the policeman there is little of that to be had in Northern Ireland.

And so it was with gratitude that we later piled into our little Volkswagen Golf and drove off the ferry at Stranraer and out into the welcoming hills of Scotland. The sun was strong, the black roads shining, and the air refreshing as it blew in through the car's open windows.

Up and over the hills we motored, on down past the lochs, across the heather-clad moors, and through the quiet Scottish towns. It was a beautiful journey, rich with the magic of the incomparable Highlands, and bursting with reminders of our Creator's might and glory. How thankful we were that we could view such sights not simply through the eyes of the wondering tourist, but as wide-eyed children, awe-struck by the sheer majesty of their Father's handiwork. And the holiday had only just begun!

Hours later, tiring now from two hundred miles of motoring, we gained our goal for that night: Inverness. Here we were to stop over with our friends David and Linda Topping, and then, with a good night's sleep behind us, we were on our way again, this time viewing the magnificent scenery to the accompaniment of some rousing Scottish music. This emanated from a cassette

David had pressed into my hand as we were taking our leave of them that morning, and with the bagpipes skirling away we were well and truly in the mood for the second leg of our Highland journey.

The port of Ullapool was our destination now, but before we could reach it the morning's sunshine was to be swallowed up in hurrying, grumbling clouds, and by the time we drove down on to the dock the car windows were up and fighting wind and rain.

'Oh, no,' moaned Clive. 'Those clouds are getting darker all the time.'

'Looks like a storm blowing up,' Keri added.

Lily scowled. 'I hope it's not going to be a rough crossing – I forgot the seasickness pills.'

'Probably just a shower,' I muttered.

But it was no such thing. Our ferry launched out into the waters of The Minch in a wind that quickly blew up into a force eight gale. Lily could have done with those pills, but then the smoke-filled lounge with its stench of spilt beer had us all feeling a bit queasy, and at the first sign of the rain letting up we staggered on deck to let the high winds and salt-spray blow the nausea away.

When at last we sighted the harbour at Stornoway we were more than ready to step on to dry land again, even though the rain was driving hard once more and the air was now quite chilly. Murdo's warm welcome on the quayside made up for it, though, and soon we were driving the short distance to the MacLeods' new bungalow where a tasty hot meal awaited us, along with the smiles of Mary and the MacLeods' youngsters, Graham and Anna-Maree.

'I thought we were all going to be blown away,' Lily laughed as we recounted the crossing.

'Aye, it can get a bit naughty out there in The Minch,' Murdo agreed. 'But it'll be fine tomorrow, just you see.'

And he was right. The following morning we awoke to find the old town bathed in a cheering golden light, and as the day progressed and we settled into our Hebridean holiday, the sun grew stronger and barely a single cloud drifted into view all day.

In fact that sun was to stay with us throughout our two weeks on the Isle of Lewis as Scotland enjoyed a rare heatwave (compensation indeed for Ibiza), so that whatever we planned – a day on the beach, a trip through the rugged beauty of the countryside, boating on the inlets and lochs – each pursuit was wrapped in blue skies and sun-tan temperatures.

There were many memorable moments, not least the occasion when (surprise, surprise!) I caught a fish. No, *four* fish, and all at the one time!

It happened during a visit we made to the home of Archie MacLeod (no relation to Murdo) in the little fishing village of Tarbert on the adjoining Isle of Harris. From here, early in the evening, Archie, Murdo, Clive and I set off in a motor-boat for the waters of The Little Minch, and there we duly paid out our lines, each with several hooks attached. Memories of that fishing trip with Clive off Donaghadee came to mind, but this time I was among friends and was not slow to ask assistance. Before long I was all geared up like a seasoned angler.

Even so, I'd not really expected to *catch* anything, but it seemed that some of the mackerel in those waters were just itching to oblige, and before I knew it a tugging on my line had me calling for more help.

'Just ease them out of the water,' Archie encouraged. 'There – what a bunch of beauties!'

I had to agree, but before I had time to appreciate the frisky little fellows on the end of my line, Murdo reminded me that the job wasn't finished until the fish were off the hooks.

'Er – *you* do it, Murdo,' I ventured (after all, *I* caught them!), and within a few moments the first fish of the evening lay in Archie's box.

'Not bad for a beginner, Dad,' chuckled Clive.

An hour or so later, with the box overflowing, we returned to Tarbert in high spirits. Clive was already speaking of his next fishing trip. This came on the following Saturday when a day's boat fishing was arranged for the young lads who attended Stornoway's YMCA. Clive was already known to the group from our previous visit and was glad of the invitation to join them. I was invited along for the ride by the group's leader, Dan MacLeman, and so with the boys piling into a hired mini-bus, and Dan and myself following by car, we set off out of Stornoway towards Marvig in the lovely lochs area of Lewis.

Brown trout was to be the hoped-for catch that day, but as we motored through the villages and out across the moorland with its occasional peat-banks and sheilings (crofters' summer shelters) Dan told me that we would first take a look at a very different fish: salmon.

'Morag, my sister-in-law, runs a salmon farm just off the shore at Marvig Bay,' he said. 'I thought you might like to take a look at it.'

The idea intrigued me, and when finally we arrived in this very lovely part of the islands Clive and I were delighted to meet Morag and her mother, Dolina MacDonald, and to have them answer our many questions about the fish they reared. Standing at the rear of their hillside home we were able to look below to where the blue-grey rock of the mountain swept down to the Atlantic, and beyond to the netted area of the salmon farm.

'You don't have far to go to work,' I joked, and Morag smiled.

'It's a good job,' she said. 'The stock has to be fed three times a day, and apart from that there's always one thing or another to tend to. It really keeps me quite busy.' She gestured towards the sea. 'Would you care for a closer look?'

Soon Morag was rowing us out across the steel-blue waters of the bay and then we were peering over the side of the boat at the bright and lively fish that were her charge.

102

'Crumbs!' exclaimed Clive. 'Fancy catching one of those!'

Morag laughed. 'Aye, they're getting a good size now.'

She told us that the salmon started off life in a hatchery from where they were moved to a cage in a fresh-water loch. After a few months they were transferred to sea water here in the bay. 'We feed them for about two years,' Morag went on, 'and harvest them when they're about fifteen pounds.'

The sight of all those fish was an inspiration to our young anglers aboard, and as soon as we'd returned Morag to the shore we struck out for a fishing ground of our own. There the lads let out their lines. As for me, I was content just to relax in the sun.

But as well as relaxation this holiday brought ample opportunity for reflection, too, and one morning, when Murdo and I strolled down to the town for a few supplies, we got talking about the situation back home in Ulster. There was much to share, what with captured rebels, legal writs and various other goings on, and Murdo was quick to express interest and concern, for as well as being a fellow Christian he is a police colleague – an Inspector with the Northern Constabulary.

Our errands that morning took us by the harbour, and with the sun streaming down to warm us we stood watching the fishing boats jostling at the quayside and the gulls hovering overhead. It was all a long, long way from the turmoil of 'Bomb City'.

'You know, Murdo,' I said, 'from here it all seems somehow unreal – the murders, the hatred, the tensions. If I didn't know better I'd think it was all a bad dream.'

He nodded, watching the Stornoway ferry nosing out to sea. 'Aye. You wonder how much longer it can go on.' Then he turned to me. 'Do you ever think you can see an end to it, Ben?'

'In God's time,' I replied. 'And we can only hope that will be soon. For some reason he's allowing us to go through these things and so there must be a purpose in it

103

all. But don't ask me what that is, for I'm not wise enough even to guess.' I paused, watching the activity on the decks of the boats below us. 'I don't know, maybe God's preparing us for something, or teaching us something. Maybe he's using the terrorist to bring us to our senses, to draw us back to himself, to make us the people he wants us to be.'

'That's a hard thing to bear,' Murdo remarked.

'Aye, it's hard, and yet all around me I see encouraging signs in people turning to Jesus Christ for forgiveness and salvation. Not just the man in the street, but the terrorist, too. Maybe that wouldn't happen if we didn't have such trials – who knows?'

Murdo said: 'True enough. But I can't say I really understand it all. And personally I'm amazed at how people like yourself cope. We have our problems here, of course, just like anywhere else, but we've nothing like the troubles in Ulster.' He fell silent for a moment, gazing out across the sun-splashed harbour. Then he said: 'Don't you ever wonder *why* Northern Ireland? History aside, I mean. Don't you ever think, what did we do to deserve this?'

I nodded. 'Well, there are those who say that what we're going through is judgment, but I think of what Jesus said when he was asked why certain people had died when a tower collapsed on them. Do you recall that incident, Murdo? He was asked, "Were these men more wicked than the rest?" And Jesus said, "No, but unless you repent you shall all likewise perish."' I turned to face my friend. 'That's how I see Ulster from *your* viewpoint, Murdo, and from the viewpoint of everyone outside the troubles. What's happening to us is not judgment, but a warning to those who are looking on to repent.'

'I've never looked at it like that,' Murdo said. 'It puts a whole new complexion on things.'

'It does. It puts the troubles in a much wider context. Sometimes I think we're inclined to look at the situation with blinkers on, seeing it from our own limited viewpoint – a human, horizontal viewpoint – but I don't think God looks at it from that angle at all. We see only the trials, but I'm sure God sees the *result* of those trials – the glorious future he's bringing us into. And if only we can get our eyes *on* that future – and I believe we can do that by faith – then we'll have a very different outlook on the day to day difficulties we have to face.'

'Aye,' said Murdo, 'it all comes down to faith in the end.'

'As long as there's faith there's hope,' I remarked. 'And I'll tell you this: after enjoying the peace of this lovely place these past days there's no way I could return to Northern Ireland without it. At times I think it's only my faith that keeps me going.'

A couple of days later, during my morning quiet time, I came across some words in the first epistle of Peter – a letter written to the early church during a time of persecution – and they seemed to sum up all that Murdo and I had been sharing down on the quayside. Encouragingly, I read: 'These trials are only to test your faith, to see whether or not it is strong and pure. It is being tested as fire tests gold and purifies it – and your faith is far more precious to God than mere gold. So if your faith remains strong after being tried in the test tube of fiery trials, it will bring you much praise and glory and honour on the day of his return.'

I shared these words with Lily later that day when we were beginning to get our things together for our departure for home the following morning. While I got out the suitcases Lily sat on the edge of the bed and read the verses for herself. When she'd finished she closed the Bible with a sigh, then looked up at me and smiled. 'Ah well – back to the test tube!' We laughed together, and then Lily said: 'It's been a lovely holiday, Ben.'

'It's been grand,' I said. 'One of the best.'

Back at home we nudged our way into the daily routine once more, our spirits refreshed and faces tanned. At least we could face the world with renewed vigour! The pressures, of course, were just the same. For me there was the return to police work, with the familiar gun on the hip and the search for bombs under the car each morning, and for both of us there was the cloud of the impending court case. There had been no developments in this area since I'd been away and there was just no telling how much longer the matter would drag on. Thankfully a telephone call from my solicitor the following week changed all that.

'Good news,' said Richard. 'We heard from the plaintiff's solicitors this morning that they're prepared to consider a settlement out of court.'

By this time I'd realised that these people were not likely to drop the issue until they'd made me put my hand in my pocket, and so Richard's news was good inasmuch that it now appeared they were having second thoughts about going to court. 'What made them change their minds?' I asked.

'Who knows?' said Richard. 'Possibly they've reconsidered the cost of failure; it was never certain that they would win. Or maybe it's because they now know that you don't have the resources for a big pay-out.'

'That's true enough.'

'Anyway,' he went on, 'I think this present situation is the best we can expect. They certainly won't drop the case. Having started the thing in motion they're obliged to look for some sort of return, if only to cover their legal expenses to date.'

'All right,' I said, 'you'd better put out some feelers and see what they would accept.'

'I'll do that. We'll start off with a token offer.'

And so it was on those grounds that a solicitors' letter went out, advising the plaintiff's solicitors that I was prepared to offer a small amount of money as a goodwill gesture. This was quickly rejected, as was a second offer, but the third proposal – offering a settlement figure of £500 – was accepted. In addition I would pay the plaintiff's legal expenses, bringing the total cost to £1,000.

There the matter came to a close. It ended, as the saying goes, not with a bang but a whimper, and I am thankful for that; it would have been a very expensive exercise. As it was, we had to scratch for the money, and for a few months afterwards the family had to tighten its belt a notch or two. But we were none the worse for that.

As for the meaning of it all – what the Lord would have us learn through it – well, that remains to be seen. Some things are clear, of course. For a start, it did not escape our notice that the total of the two sums of money I paid out – a thousand pounds each to Claire and solicitors – was matched by Judy's gift towards the ministry of *Hope in 'Bomb City'*. And to this day the light that both Judy and Claire brought into my life during that dark time continues to encourage and inspire when the going gets tough.

Equally, I am heartened as I reflect on the way in which Lily and I saw the Lord proving to us yet again that he is as good as his word. 'He will supply all your needs' was the promise he had given us, and that proved wonderfully true. For over the weeks and months following the completion of the case, many kind and loving people sent us gifts, some small, some large, but all unsolicited. We had asked for prayer, but never money, yet God, we believe, moved upon those dear people to stand with us not only spiritually but practically. The result was that our loving and faithful Father brought back to us the money that we had paid out. Every last penny.

The best return to come out of all this, however, was from the investment made by Judy in those books. They went out, as she'd requested, to schools, hospitals, army camps and prisons, and over the years since then we have been privileged to learn of some of the ways in which God has honoured that gift and multiplied it in terms of blessing to the people who received a free copy. Often this insight has come through letters, and perhaps

107

one will suffice to illustrate the point. This came from an army major and ran as follows:

'Dear Lady, I have been told that you have paid for my copy of *Hope in 'Bomb City'* (amongst many others). Apart from thanking you, I would like to tell you what a loving and valuable investment this has been. I am a serviceman who has seen service in Belfast, as have many of my friends. The news and impressions which we receive from the Province are inevitably pessimistic, and it is so good to hear some Good News of the Lord's work there. I have lent the book to many of my friends and their wives, and they in turn will pass it on.

'For me personally, I am encouraged and strengthened by you. I know a little of your own loss and sadness, and to think that you have emerged from that still proclaiming our Lord and giving to his work fills me with wonder at the power and love of Jesus.

'Thank you, and my love in Christ's name.'

This letter, I believe, represents only a fraction of the good things God has done, and continues to do, through those specially purchased books. After all, if he can bring so much blessing out of just one copy, who knows what he can achieve through the other 2,249! At that I can only guess. But what I know for certain is that Judy made the very best kind of investment with her money, for she translated it into the currency of God's kingdom. And for that she'll have treasure in heaven.

10: Death of a friend

It was a Saturday in mid-November and winter was beginning to bite, yet in the main office at Knock Police Headquarters the atmosphere was warm and humming with lively banter. Morale was high – for myself I was glad not to be needed at Castlereagh for interviews that morning – and with the prospect of a fairly easy day ahead of us we were quick to join in with my colleague Brian's ribbing of certain officers' golf handicaps. I threw in my own two pennyworth with a crack about preferring a good, hard game of squash, and suggesting that golf was really more suited to the elderly. This kept the laughter rolling a bit longer, but sooner or later we had to come down to earth.

'Quiet, boys!' Frank, our Detective Chief Inspector, had the telephone to his ear, listening intently, and his face showed disbelief and shock. Instantly the banter died away and every head turned to await the bad news.

The phone went down and Frank sprang to his feet, his colour drained, his voice taut. 'Robert Bradford and another man have been murdered at Finaghy Community Centre. Get over there as quick as you can.'

Sheer horror shot us out of our seats and sent us dashing for the door. Robert Bradford, Official Unionist MP and one of the leading figures in Ulster politics, *dead*!

In the speeding car the shock set in and our minds raced wildly. The gunmen had got themselves a big one this time.

Some would say it was hardly surprising; that a man of such prominence who was also an outspoken critic of the IRA was a certain target, and that it had been only a matter of time before he was silenced. But as we sped through the streets of Belfast to the scene of his murder, such considerations began to fade. Almost certainly it *was* a political assassination, but uppermost in my mind was the death of a friend.

I had known the Rev. Robert Bradford for many years and had occasionally shared the platform with him at Christian meetings. Though much of his time was now taken up with his work as a politician, his faith continued to be the driving force of his life and he had remained eager to accept invitations to witness to his faith or to proclaim his Saviour at church services and rallies. I was always glad when such occasions brought us together, for Robert was a fine, godly man and his warm smile and gentle manner made him a pleasure to be with.

Now my friend was dead. And, as we soon discovered, he had died as he had lived – in the service of the people. On many Saturday mornings he had held a people's clinic here at the community centre in Finaghy – a regular 'surgery' where he met with his constituents and sought to help them in their various problems. Despite frequent threats and attempts on his life he had continued to make himself available to anyone who thought he could be of assistance to them.

But on this sharp November morning, sitting in his dark woollen overcoat at his usual makeshift desk in a side room of the centre, the gunmen got their wish and removed him from this earthly scene with several bullets in the head. Posing as decorators in boiler-suits, and carrying a workman's plank to aid their trickery, three IRA terrorists took the lone police guard at the door by surprise. Two of them then ran through the building, throwing open one door after another until they found their prey. In the main hall, children attending a young-sters' disco ran screaming and diving for cover. Seated opposite Robert at his table were an elderly couple asking his advice. They barely had chance to turn before the act of murder was done.

Outside the killers raced from the scene, having also shot dead caretaker Ken Campbell. They got clean away.

Now, only minutes later, and with a police incident room already established and inquiries underway, I stood alone in the blood-spattered room, staring at the repulsive aftermath and fighting a sudden anger. Such a good man; such a wicked waste of life. I would surely do all within my power to help bring those responsible to justice.

Then, strangely, the frustration I felt melted away as I became aware of a calmness in that room. It was not simply a stillness – the stillness of death which I have experienced at the scene of many murders – but a living peace. Suddenly, and quite forcibly, it came to me: Robert is with the Lord. A scripture drifted into mind. 'Jesus Christ in your heart is your only hope of glory.'

The longer I looked at Robert's stilled features the stronger the impression grew. At this very moment my friend was with his Saviour! Robert, through Jesus Christ, had attained glory. The terrorists had done their worst – and Robert had been ushered into the best.

I turned towards the door, sensing the power of my own faith strong within me. What did that verse in Romans say? 'Living or dying we follow the Lord – either way we are his.' It was a moment of rare clarity, of divine reality. The Christian just cannot lose!

But these thoughts would have to wait. Turning to the job in hand, I noted what I needed to note for the purposes of the official inquiry and headed out of the door.

There were many witnesses to these crimes, including a number of young children, and the following hours were spent taking statements. This was largely a matter of following routine, and yet I have always found that when kiddies are involved the issues are somehow thrown into a more tragic perspective, highlighting the insanity that has now become an all-too-familiar part of the world these young lives have inherited. That day, as always, I found it very disturbing that even one of our nation's young ones should be subjected to the terror of the gunmen, and for their sakes I was saddened.

One such child was little Ann, aged six. Having witnessed the violence she was too afraid to answer the door when Eddie and I called later that afternoon, crying out, 'Who's there?' – frightened in case it was someone come to do her harm, and needing her mother's reassurance.

Then there was three-year-old Emma who was held in her mother's arms as she told us what she had seen. 'Ken Campbell shot dead – bang, bang.'

What effect such experiences will have on these young minds does not bear thinking about.

But on this day it was not just the children who were shocked. As word of the murders spread through the community and then the country, expressions of horror came from every quarter. Robert Bradford was a popular public figure, well liked by many and respected by even more, and throughout the Province all right-thinking people were grief-stricken. Some were angry, too, which was understandable, but after the shouts of condemnation from politicians and church leaders through the media there followed a more unnerving sound – the sound of the war-cry. Talk of retaliation, of vigilante patrols, of civil war was rife, and within a few short hours the community was gripped by much restlessness and tension. Many more heated words were to follow, culminating in the proposal of a 'third force' – a body of armed citizens who would take the battle on to the streets and rout the IRA once and for all.

Before the day was out, a young Roman Catholic man had been shot dead on his doorstep. The motive? What did it matter. It was simply another act of evil to contend with; another outrage calling for heartfelt sympathy towards the victim's family and friends.

In the midst of all this violence it was refreshing and encouraging to witness the gentle yet strong spirit of Robert's widow, Norah, and to hear her express her deep-seated peace and faith in Jesus Christ as she was interviewed on the TV news that same evening. Of her husband she said, 'I believe Robert did a tremendous amount of good and just hope that some good will come out of all this. As for the killers, the Lord will deal with them in his own good time.'

Her words of faith were a flash of light in a very dark day, a day that kept me busy on the case until late at night. When finally I returned home it had gone eleven o'clock and I was dog-tired. There wasn't even the hoped-for consolation of a day off tomorrow; such a case demanded that the department pull out all the stops and for days to come we would be working long hours.

The next morning, listening to the news as I shaved, I felt further vibrations of Ulster's unrest reverberating through the air waves as more reaction to the murders was reported, and I was glad when the news finished and gave way to Margaret Mooney's record request programme. 'Reflections', as it is called, focuses on hymns and gospel songs and is often an inspiration to me as it lifts my thoughts to a higher plane. On this particular morning one of the pieces chosen was 'Precious Memories', and it was with this song flowing through the house that I left to take Shane for an early morning walk before heading out to work.

Precious memories . . .

At such times it is good to remember. When there is civil disquiet, and when one's personal peace is being challenged, it is good to reflect on those things which have proved to be a source of strength in past trials.

That's how it must have been for Robert, I mused as Shane and I reached the fields; it was the victory of Jesus Christ in his heart that had kept him going, knowing that the God who had seen him through yesterday's storms would not fail him today.

And yet, as Robert and I both knew, that was only one side of the coin. As I stood watching Shane bounding through the long grass, the coin flipped over.

'What is faith? It is the confident assurance that something we want is going to happen. It is the certainty that what we hope for is waiting for us, even though we cannot see it ahead.'

A while later, as we made for home, I set to thinking about these things and wondered what Robert had 'hoped for'. Peace in Northern Ireland would have been at the top of his priorities, of course, but equally he had been involved in seeking to bring about so many other changes for good in the community.

At the same time, I knew, Robert had had his sights fixed on a higher goal. And back indoors, turning to that chapter on faith in Hebrews, I read words that seemed to say so much about this man and his aspirations, and the fact that his life had been so tragically cut short.

'These men of faith . . . died without ever receiving all that God had promised them; but they saw it all awaiting them ahead and were glad, for they agreed that this earth was not their real home but that they were just strangers visiting down here.'

The strength of Robert's faith was echoed the following Tuesday at his funeral. Here, and at memorial services held simultaneously all over the Province, the many thousands of mourners heard these words: 'The one thing which made him what he was, was his saving faith in Jesus Christ our Lord. His conversion was the foundation of his life of service.' The tribute went on, 'He has gone from us like a valiant for the trust to the Father's house. If we would follow him there, we too must have our faith in the Saviour.'

The following day this tribute, along with extensive coverage of the memorial services, was printed in the *News Letter*, our morning newspaper.

'Did you see this?' asked Lily, handing me the paper after tea that evening. 'There are some encouraging words there, all about faith and such.'

I read the tribute through, then smiled. 'Faith in "Bomb City",' I said. 'I hope people sit up and take notice.' I returned the paper to her and she stood looking at it, wistful. 'What's on your mind?'

'Norah,' she said simply. 'I hope she'll be all right. And their little girl – what's her name? Claire, isn't it?'

'That's it. She's six – or is it seven? I can't remember.'

'So young,' said Lily.

'Aye.'

We both knew that the Lord would take care of them, but even so it was so sad for such a wee girl to lose her daddy.

'Will you get a chance to call in and see them, Ben?'

'I expect so,' I replied. 'There are bound to be a few loose ends to tie up with Norah. But that will have to wait for the present. I'll let you know when it might be, love. Maybe you'd like to come along.'

It was another ten days before I was free enough to visit Norah Bradford at her home in South Belfast. I needed to speak to her about some of Robert's personal possessions and one or two police matters, and after telephoning from home one lunchtime to let her know that we were on our way, Lily and I drove to her lovely bungalow in Newforge Lane.

It had been less than a month since I'd last seen Norah. That was at an evangelistic mission in Finaghy where we had spent quite some time chatting at the close of the service. At that time she had been bright-eyed and relaxed. Now, as Lily and I walked up the path, I wondered what sort of toll the tragedy had taken. But as the door opened and Norah appeared with a welcoming smile, I knew immediately that she was enjoying God's peace.

'Come on in,' she greeted. 'I've just put the kettle on.'

Over coffee, and with Robert's Yorkshire terriers, Bo and Towser, scampering in and out of the kitchen, I quickly cleared the business I'd come about. Our talk of Robert, however, went on, and Lily and I were pleased to witness the evidence of the many prayers that we knew were still being offered up for Norah and Claire every day. There had been difficult times, she told us, and she still shed many tears, but it was at those times that she realised just how close the Lord was, and how caring, even in the little things.

'On the day Robert died,' she said, 'a single white blossom appeared on our tree out in the front garden, and that meant a lot to me.' She turned to Lily. 'There was only one leaf left on that tree, you see, and we thought it was finished for the year – but then . . . well, I just knew it was from the Lord.'

'A sign of new life,' Lily remarked, and Norah smiled.

'That's a great comfort,' she said, 'to know that Robert lives on in God's presence.'

I appreciated the sentiment and sat vaguely remembering those verses about faith, and about God's people being no more than strangers visiting down here. 'Do you feel that Robert's work was finished, Norah?' I asked.

She didn't hesitate. 'I do, Ben. I remember being asked about his work as an MP just prior to his last re-election to Westminster, and I said then that I believed Robert was there for a purpose, and that until that was finished the Lord would look after him.' She smiled. 'Our God doesn't make mistakes, does he?'

'That's for sure,' I said.

She took our cups and refilled them, her thoughts far away. After a pause she said, 'Do you know, at the end of that day I did what I never thought I would be able to do. I thanked God – thanked him for allowing that day.' Her eyes were full. 'Perhaps some people wouldn't understand that, but it was just there in my heart. I told him that I didn't understand *why* it had happened, but all the

116

same I knew he wanted me to trust him, and that meant thanking him for his perfect will.'

I opened my mouth to speak but said nothing, for suddenly I was deeply aware of Norah's grief and knew that at this point words would be meaningless. Perhaps I was beginning to learn that at such times it is far more helpful just to listen.

In the pause Norah sat dabbing at her eyes with a handkerchief and I busied myself stirring my coffee. At last Norah said, 'The worst day so far has been the Saturday after it happened. That was a really bad day, I'm afraid. I went to the cemetery – in search of some sort of understanding, I suppose – and I just couldn't stop crying. The wreaths were still there – my own, the little bunch of flowers Claire had picked from her granny's garden, and many more – and I just wept.' She paused, composing herself. 'But then the most wonderful thing happened – the Lord spoke to me. It must have been him, for I was completely alone.'

'You heard a voice?' Lily asked.

'A whisper,' she replied. 'He said, "As Judas Iscariot had a part to play in the crucifixion of the Lord Jesus Christ but was insignificant in my final plan, so the terrorists had a part to play in Robert's death but are as unimportant to my mighty purposes."' She smiled reflectively. 'I still had tears in my eyes when I left, but they were tears of joy.'

I smiled with her. 'That's a precious memory, Norah.'

'Very precious,' she said. 'Isn't our Lord wonderful?'

We shared other memories that day, too, for as we got talking about other things I reminded Norah of the conversation we'd had the last time we'd met, after the service at Finaghy. On that occasion we had discovered that she and I had shared the same hometown as children – Portadown. Norah's father, I learned, had been the Methodist minister there for a while, and though our paths had never crossed we discovered that

117

we both remembered the same names and faces from those distant years.

Sitting there in Norah's kitchen, looking out upon the lovely views of the Lagan valley, we pulled a few more memories out of the hat and thus provoked a laugh or two.

And it was on that happy note, an hour or so later, that we parted. Norah had to collect Claire from school and I had things to do in the office. But though we had to go our separate ways, the memories we'd shared lingered on.

I well remembered the Methodist Church at Portadown, for as a teenager I had spent many happy hours involved in one or other of the various activities that took place there. The Christian Endeavour group, the Sunday afternoon Bible class, the male voice choir, the social evenings and film shows . . . I was involved in all of these, along with many other young people, and looking back on those times I am thankful that my life had been so full.

But there was another reason why I was not likely to forget my participation in events at the Methodist Church, for it was during a film show in the church hall one Saturday night that the course of my life was to change. For some reason my thoughts that evening were towards the police force – something I'd given a lot of thought over the months – and sitting there in the darkness, my eyes on the screen but my mind elsewhere, I prayed that I might become a policeman.

Of course, no one could have realised what that would mean in years to come; no one could have guessed that within a decade our country would see the start of such a violent and prolonged campaign of terror, or that within two decades the RUC would become the most besieged police force in the world with its members being given only a fifty-fifty chance of reaching retirement. But even if I'd known I don't think my prayer would have been any different. Nor do I now regret the choice I made, knowing what I now know and seeing what I have seen. For though the path has been littered with tragedy and trial, it has also been sweet with the presence of a loving God who does not remain aloof from the problems that beset his children, but who stoops down and draws alongside . . . and travels with them all the way home.

Robert had proved that love for himself. Norah, too. And in days to come, I was sure, she and young Claire would prove it over and over again.

Heading back down into Belfast that afternoon, dropping Lily off and returning to the murder case, I felt strangely optimistic. Even though the shock-waves of Robert's death were still being felt across the community, and doubtless would continue to cause ripples for some time to come, I had seen within Norah the irrepressible hope and peace of the Saviour whose power always shines brightest when the storm hits hardest. As long as I saw such a victorious response to the evil inflicted upon our people, I mused, I too would have cause for faith in 'Bomb City'.

I turned the car along the Ormeau Embankment into Ravenhill Road, and there the words of Jesus came to me: 'Here on earth you will have many trials and sorrows; but take courage, I have overcome the world.'

With a prayer of thanks on my lips, I swung the car through the gates of police headquarters and went back to work.

Postscript

'Hurry, son,' calls Dad from the foot of the stairs. 'The train will not wait for a couple of stragglers.'

'I'm coming, I'm coming,' I cry, scooping my pocket money off the dresser and snatching up my cap. Then I'm clattering down the stairs, leaping the last three, kissing Mum and falling out into the street where Dad is already away to the station.

The tickets are barely in our hands before we hear the hiss and clatter of the great engine pulling into Portadown, and together we rush for the platform and fling ourselves into the carriage, collapsing on the worn seats.

The whistle blows and I drop the window to watch the charges of steam burst into the morning air and drift away on the playful breeze. Soon we are moving, and the steam, unleashed, is towering into the blue. The steady chug-chugging accelerates, the engine brass glints in the early sun, and the 8.15 goes snaking and clanking on its way.

It is the start of a great adventure. We have our sandwiches in a brown paper bag, our plastic macs for the sudden summer shower, and all the wonder a small boy can use. We are on our way to The Free State.

Warrenpoint is our destination this fine morning, and when finally the mighty, puffing beast crawls into the seaside town there is a smile upon our lips and in our eyes. Stepping from the train I am sure I can already smell the salt-spray mingling with the heady aroma of coal smoke and engine oil . . . or is that just a wee boy's anticipation?

Through the barrier and out into the street we go, fond memories of a previous visit guiding our steps as we make for the sea-front.

'Look, Dad, there's the fair! Can we go on the dodgems – *please*?'

'Aye,' says Dad, grinning at his son's pleasure and reaching into his pocket. 'But just the one go, mind.'

Once is enough to refresh the memory of the bumping and bone-jarring, and to fuel this part of the tale that tomorrow will have the Jeffers boys and Bobby McNally wide-eyed back home.

Then it's off along the sea-front, past the stately pier and the open-air swimming pool, and down on the beach to paddle on the edge of Carlingford Lough and skim flat pebbles across the water.

With the sun high and the sea breeze strong, we sit and dive into the sandwiches, looking out across the sea to the green pastures and craggy mountains of another country.

'We'll get the motor-boat soon as we've eaten,' says Dad.

I have been before, but it is no less an adventure, and I sit pondering the mystery of a foreign country that looks just like our own.

The fare for the crossing is one and sixpence – a bit expensive, says Dad, who's sure the price has almost doubled since our last visit, but as we've come this far . . .

The little boat cuts out into the lough, its engine buzzing, and me with my hand trailing in the water at the prow.

'Can we have an ice-cream when we get there, Dad?'

His big hand rests on my shoulder and he smiles, nodding.

The boat slows, the engine splutters and dies as we drift the final yards to shore. There are customs men here at Omeath, and the police officers wear different uniforms from across the water. It is indeed a foreign land.

We pass through the checkpoint and walk slowly, dreamily up the street. There's the ice-cream shop. 'Two threepenny cones, please.' We walk on, gazing into shop windows and pausing at the market stalls. Soon the ices are but a memory.

At the top of the street, waiting to whisk trippers into the countryside, are the brightly-painted jaunting cars with their big, powerful horses dozing in the midday heat.

'Let's take a ride,' Dad ventures generously, his hand moving to his pocket once more.

Soon we are up in the car with its back-to-back seats, riding out along the shore road, the lough below us, the mountains climbing at our backs.

'Where are we going, Dad?'

'A little place called Calvary,' he replies, his hair fluffing in the breeze.

'Calvary?'

The jaunting car creaks rhythmically, in time with the clip-clopping of the horse's hooves on the coal-black road. Down at the water's edge a mallard is startled from the reeds and takes to the wing.

'Aye. It's one of the local beauty spots.'

This does not excite a small boy. 'Are there any shops there? I want to get some of that American bubble gum.' Such a treat is not available at home.

'Well, that'll have to come out of *your* pocket.' He falls silent again, looking around at the great beauty that only he sees. Then he turns and looks at me, grinning his funny grin. 'I don't know if there are shops there, son, but if not we'll build some before we leave. Is that all right?'

'Long as they sell bubble gum,' I reply.

Hours later, when the sun is low, we climb aboard the steam train again, our pockets empty but hearts full. We have a gift for Mum, some sweets for Leah, and a whole bunch of memories.

It has been a grand day. We have been to Southern Ireland, to The Free State. A small boy who is fast falling asleep on his father's lap thinks it is fun down on the border.

Alas, today it is a very different story. So much has changed. Take Warrenpoint. Though still an attractive seaside town, the name now holds a more bitter memory as the place where eighteen British soldiers died in an IRA booby-trap explosion.

And then there's the border itself. Long gone are the boyhood dreams; now the border symbolises other, darker things. For members of the RUC it is a dangerous place to be. For the terrorist, trying to resurrect a long-ago war, it is the motivation to kill innocent people.

But if only the gunmen would realise it, there's no future in the past. This world with all its territorial squabbles is destined for the scrap-heap in God's mighty, eternal plan – it's there for all to see in his book – and in that coming day, when Ulster and Ireland are but a vague recollection, who will be able to say that the slaughter and the bloodshed were worthwhile? In God's new heaven and new earth there will be no Irish tricolour, no Union Jack – only the standard of the one who poured out his life to bring men peace with God: the Lord Jesus Christ. His kingdom is the only one that will last, the only one worth fighting for. If a man wants a cause that's worth living for – even dying for – let him enlist in the Lord's army.

Who am I to make such bold pronouncements? Just a forgiven sinner. I have been to Calvary, you see – not just the one in Ireland in search of bubble gum, but the Calvary where God's Son forever awaits us with arms outstretched in forgiveness and reconciliation to the Father. There he won my heart, and now my life is his.

But I don't delude myself. Like St Paul, 'I am still not all I should be, but I am bringing all my energies to bear on this one thing: *forgetting the past* and looking forward to all that lies ahead, I strain to reach the end of the race and receive the prize for which God is calling us up to heaven because of what Christ Jesus did for us.'

124

This is not some sort of spiritual anaesthetic; the hope of tomorrow does not deaden the pain of today. The troubles are real and you and I must endure them. But we need not endure them alone.

Recently I read of a little girl lying in a hospital bed, gradually losing her sight. Day by day her world grew darker, and soon fear seized her young heart. Towards the end, when blindness was almost upon her, she was visited by Pastor Sangster. As panic gripped her, the little girl cried out, 'O Dr Sangster, God has taken away my sight.'

The famous preacher took her hand and leaned over her, speaking tenderly. 'Don't let him take it, child – give it to him.'

The great darkness that threatens to engulf us in Northern Ireland may not go away, but it will be robbed of its terror if we give it to God. He can handle what we can't, and is longing to do just that for each one of us. He is the God who knows me through and through, who loves me as I am, and who wants to carry my burden. The same is true for you.

Don't let him take it – *give it to him*.

When we do this, we find not only that our load is lightened, but also that our trials are put into God's perspective. And it is on this note that I wish to close this book, and this series of books, pointing you to Jesus, the only truly satisfying source of hope, love and faith in 'Bomb City', and affirming my belief that the best is yet to come. The assurance is there in the Word of God:

'These troubles and sufferings of ours are, after all, quite small and won't last very long. Yet this short time of distress will result in God's richest blessing upon us for ever and ever.

'So we do not look at what we can see at this moment, the troubles all around us, but we look forward to the joys in heaven which we have not yet seen.

'The troubles will soon be over, but the joys to come will last for ever.'

Besides ministering to people through his books Ben Forde also reaches out to people through his music.

Having enjoyed reading this book you will be interested to know of Ben's latest record.

BEN FORDE
My Peace

Having served in Northern Ireland's RUC as a Police Officer in the C.I.D. over fifteen years of terrorism, peace is something Ben has pursued and worked hard at. Many of the songs on this album refer to the deeper peace which is only found through trusting in Jesus Christ. £5.25

3 Beggarwood Lane, Basingstoke, Hants RG23 7LP.

If you have enjoyed reading this book and would like to see our complete catalogue, ask at your nearest Christian bookshop for one or write directly to MARSHALL PICKERING COMMUNICATIONS at the address below.

If you have ideas for new Christian books or other products please write to us too!

MARSHALL PICKERING COMMUNICATIONS
3 Beggarwood Lane
Basingstoke
Hants RG23 7LP
England